What's Your Sports IQ?

The Unofficial Guide to Sports Literacy

By
Bill Jeakle and Ed Wyatt

Illustrations by
Philip Chalk

A PLUME BOOK

PLUME
Published by the Penguin Group
Penguin Books USA Inc., 375 Hudson Street,
New York, New York 10014, U.S.A.
Penguin Books Ltd, 27 Wrights Lane,
London W8 5TZ, England
Penguin Books Australia Ltd, Ringwood,
Victoria, Australia
Penguin Books Canada Ltd, 10 Alcorn Ave.,
Toronto, Ontario, Canada M4V 3B2
Penguin Books (N.Z.) Ltd, 182-190 Wairau Road,
Auckland 10, New Zealand
Penguin Books Ltd, Registered Offices:
Harmondsworth, Middlesex, England

First published by Plume, an imprint of New American
Library, a division of Penguin Books USA Inc.

 PLUME TRADEMARK REG. U.S. PAT. OFF. AND FOREIGN
COUNTRIES REGISTERED TRADEMARK—MARCA REGISTRADA

ISBN 0-452-26693-9
Designed by Jeakle/Wyatt Productions

First Printing, October, 1991
10 9 8 7 6 5 4 3 2 1

PRINTED IN THE UNITED STATES OF AMERICA

Photo Credits

p26—Heisman: Downtown Athletic Club
p28—Joe Namath: New York Jets
p29—OJ Simpson: Buffalo Bills
p30—Chuck Bednarik: Philadelphia Eagles
p30—Lou Holtz: U. Notre Dame
p34—John Elway: Stanford Univ.
p43—Phog Allen: Kansas Univ.
p45—Michael Jordan: Chicago Bulls
p46—Jerry West: LA Lakers
p47—Magic Johnson: LA Lakers
p48—John Wooden: UCLA
p49—Dean Smith: Univ of N. Carolina
p50—Wilt Chamberlain: LA Lakers
p51—Hank Luisetti: Stanford Univ.
p54—Kareem Abdul-Jabbar: LA Lakers
p57—Dick Vitale: ESPN
p66—Ty Cobb: Detroit Tigers
p67—Ted Williams: Boston Red Sox
p68—Billy Martin: New York Yankees
p69—Lou Gehrig: New York Yankees
p70—Joe DiMaggio: New York Yankees
p94—Pebble Beach: USGA
p95—Cherry Hills: USGA
p96—Bobby Jones: USGA
p96—Ben Hogan: USGA
p97—Arnold Palmer: USGA
p97—Jack Nicklaus: USGA
p106—Bjorn Borg: IMG
p107—Billie Jean King: IMG
p107—Martina Navratilova: IMG
p116—Dale Earnhardt: Darlington Raceway
p126—Iditarod: Alaska Division of Tourism
p129—John Thompson: Georgetown Univ.
p132—Bobby Knight: Indiana University
p133—Adolph Rupp: Univ of Kentucky
p134—Johnny Unitas: Indianapolis Colts
p135—Wade Boggs: Boston Red Sox
p141—Wrestling: Oklahoma Univ.
p146—Wyoming stadium: Univ. of Wyoming
p150—Roger Clemens: Boston Red Sox
p151—Bo Jackson: Downtown Athletic Club
p152—Joe Paterno: Penn State Univ.
p152—Knute Rockne: Univ. of Notre Dame
p153—Michael Jordan: Chicago Bulls
p153—Bill Walton: UCLA
p154—Magic Johnson: LA Lakers
p155—Babe Ruth: New York Yankees
p157—Ivan Lendl: IMG
p158—Darlington 500: Darlington International Raceway
p159—Chris Berman: ESPN
p159—Tiger Stadium: Detroit Tigers

Acknowledgements

The authors would like to thank the following people for their involvement in the production of this book: Steve Nieswander for writing and layout, Dave Hill for research, Mike Flake for layout, Brad Peterson, Dan Merchant, David High at The Computer Store, Steve Weaver, Joe Piscatella, Clark Beyer, Steve Anstett, Hugh and Connie Wyatt, Ed and Nancy Jeakle, Romney Wyatt, Bill Nye the Science Guy, Jim Baumann, Steve Zansberg, Rick Dujmov, the people at Turner Broadcasting, KOIN-TV, KING-TV, Pete Ferren at QFC, and Gilles Desjardins at Le Groupe Videotron. Finally, thanks to Rosemary Ahern, Arnold Dolin, and all the people at Plume Books.

Contents

1 Introduction

Introduction

Sports and games play a large part in the lifestyle and psyche of everyday America. Every week, 101,000 people pack the University of Michigan's football stadium to watch their beloved Wolverines. Major league baseball's Los Angeles Dodgers see more than three million people pass through their turnstiles every season. Pro basketball's Michael Jordan makes millions endorsing Nike shoes, Wheaties, and a number of other products; he's more visible than the President.

But what if you don't like sports? What if you think it's insane to paint your face and scream at a TV camera like a deranged lunatic, or what if watching a 300-pound guy with a gut hanging over a pair of tight satin pants isn't your idea of a good time? Then sports have no effect on your life and you can just sit back and pretend they don't even exist, right?

Wrong! Because unless you're a social misfit who abhors the thought of interacting with anyone else, or you live in a self-contained world like the Boy in the Bubble, sports in some way will enter into your life. Hell, the Boy in the Bubble probably had cable.

If you want an example, just look at the business world. Here's the scenario: a group of high-level managers get together at a sales conference. They have outlined a program with titles like "Winning" and "The Competitive Edge." They hire a motivational speaker to kick off the event—Notre Dame football coach Lou Holtz, for instance—and his talk focuses on the value of teamwork and setting goals.

After the speech, everyone breaks into groups to create a presentation on different aspects of the company. Each group presents its findings to the others. The presentations are compared, rated, and ranked.

Later that night, after golf or tennis, the managers gather to hobnob, and the buzzwords start to fly. Listen to the jargon of the business world and you'll hear terms like "team player," "level playing field," and "doing some blocking." You don't have to look far to find sports analogies flowing from achievement-oriented managers. Somehow, sports find their way into most situations in life.

Two trends have pushed athletics to the fore in our society. The first, obviously, is television. Each channel now needs to fill over 8,000 hours of programming per year, and only so much of that can be home shopping channels or dance shows with low-angle shots of teenage girls. Sports—even obscure sports like Australian rules football and windsurfing—tend to attract viewers not interested in other forms of programming. The average household has the television on more than seven hours a day, so more time is spent watching sports events than ever before.

Second, because of the escalating rights fees paid to teams and athletes as a result of so many TV viewers, professional athletes have become de facto business leaders, making huge salaries, endorsing products, and making speeches to business audiences. And, now that many great athletic performers are given the opportunity to attend college, they continue to be leaders after their athletic careers are over. Jack Kemp, Bill Bradley, Roger Staubach, Dave Bing, and Julius Erving have learned that there is life beyond athletics.

So with the great athlete and coach exalted, and the world becoming more and more enamored of sports teams and sports paraphernalia, being Sports Literate is more important than ever. You don't have to be a sports nut, with a football lamp, a college mascot trash can, and an office painted Carolina blue. But in the '90s, with the focus on achievement and competition, a knowledge of the rudiments of sport is assumed and just might pull you past the "glass ceiling," that invisible barrier to advancement that you can't quite see or feel, but you suspect is there.

The good news is that you don't really need to know a lot to be Sports Literate. Let's face it, some of the most knowledgeable sports people in the world aren't the most intellectual. Sure, Pat Haden was a Rhodes scholar, but there isn't much brilliance in John Madden's "Pow! Ooh! Bang!" commentaries, or Dick Vitale's "Gotta give up the rock!" rants. You can learn just a few choice names, statistics, and questions and you'll be able to fool most of the sports experts most of the time.

You'll need to know the most about the key sports: football (college and pro), basketball (college and pro), baseball, tennis, and golf. After that, you can get by with just key words or phrases, like "Hey, stop high sticking The Great One" (hockey), or "I can't believe he's making a pit stop" (auto racing).

How to Fake It

The first step to becoming Sports Literate is to realize that you may never be Sports Fluent. The goal should be to understand and get by in the language of sport, even though you might not feel comfortable speaking that language. Do what you have to do to raise your Sports IQ enough to get by.

You know the old ploy. Can't dance? Join the band. Don't drink? Volunteer to bartend. Sports Illiterate? Take the reins of the conversation yourself. Just reach into the grab bag of Sports Controversies and sit back and watch. Try one of these.

Pro Football

> "You know, I really don't think Joe Montana is all that great."

College Football

> "You know, they say that Notre Dame has a clean program, but with all those years of winning, there's got to be a recruiting violation or two somewhere."

The trick is to take a sacred institution of the sport, such as Joe Montana or Notre Dame, and call their ability/integrity into question. You'll tap into a vein of Sports Truth: on every sports issue, the ratio between cynics and idolizers is 50/50. A great question will bring out the division. Let's try a few more.

Pro Basketball

"I think Magic Johnson is a crybaby."

Soccer

"Soccer players are wimps."

Baseball

"Jose Canseco sucks!"

Whoops! You made an error common to the not yet Sports Literate. Your Canseco observation impugns a negative figure, and is therefore true rather than argumentative. A better example might be:

"Harry Caray sucks!"

Now, you've got an argument! The venerable Chicago announcer is revered by Cubbies fans, but can get under the skin of any redblooded St. Louis Cardinal supporter. To keep your momentum going, make sure that your interlocutors are served plenty of beer and salty food, so that they gradually forget that you're not saying anything as their statements get more and more outrageous. If you're at the office, you won't need the beer. The prospect of killing an hour with a good Sports Controversy should do the trick.

Sports Scenarios

You'll find numerous occasions throughout the course of a typical business day when sports terms are used. Make sure you recognize these sports scenarios and what they mean.

•**Scenario 1:** Tim, a television executive, asks his partner Vanessa about a new TV series called *London Cops*. Vanessa smiles broadly and says, *"It's a slam dunk!"*

Sports Allusion: *Slam dunk:* The coolest play in basketball, ramming the ball viciously through the hoop.

Translation: The show is great, a potential hit.

•**Scenario 2:** Harrison, a corporate executive, has to fire an employee who isn't working out. As part of his evaluation, Harrison comments that the employee *"just isn't a team player."*

Sports Allusion: *Team player:* Someone out for himself, not dedicated to a team goal.

Translation: The employee didn't care about the company.

•**Scenario 3:** Pete, an ad agency account manager, hasn't found anything out about the Microtech account. Pete's boss says he needs to find out, and tells Pete to *"apply the full court press."*

Sports Allusion: *Full court press:* In basketball, when the defense goes all out to try and make the offense turn the ball over.

Translation: Do everything you can to find out about the account.

To use another sports allusion, the ball's now in your court. Turn these pages and be well on your way to Sports Literacy. Each of the following sections is divided into main facts, how to watch a game, legends, the fans and players you'll see, film classics, an insider quiz, and a glossary. Some of the information will be a little tough if the sport is new to you. Don't worry about it. Pick up a tidbit or two and try it out at the office. Remember to keep this book handy in case a conversation turns to arcane sports trivia. A quick scan of the glossary should bail you out.

Which Are You?

Sports Ignorant: You have no idea who the Mets or the Yankees are, and you think Bo Jackson had blond dreadlocks and tempted Dudley Moore in the movie *10*. You often try to mask your ignorance by pronouncing sports as "trivial" and "games for immature men." You are not well liked by the majority of Americans.

Sports Know-It-All: You know the starting defensive line-up for the Birmingham Americans of the long- defunct World Football League. You missed the birth of your child because a re-run of the Lakers-Pistons championship game was on. At parties you are a bore.

Sports Literate: You move with ease through all circles of society, knowing just enough to ingratiate yourself, but not too much to offend. You have opinions on Pete Rose and Jerry Tarkanian, but you don't watch every Arena Football game. You are a welcome guest at any party.

2

Football

Football

Football is the most popular sport in America.

As a Sports Literate fan, you'll need to know about professional and college football. College football has been around since 1869, when Princeton and Rutgers played the first game. It enjoyed immense popularity around the turn of the century, before President Theodore Roosevelt threatened to ban the game because of excessive violence. New rules were introduced in 1906 and today the college game has regained its popularity and, as evidenced by massive television contracts, will continue to boom.

The professional game began in the 1920s, and played little brother to the colleges for many years. In the 1960s, professional football surged with the inception of the Super Bowl (1967). The sport grew steadily from that point on. Today, the NFL is an American institution. It dominates Sunday morning and afternoon television viewing, especially among middle-aged males. ABC's *Monday Night Football* has been a solid fixture since 1971.

Professional Football

The National Football League (NFL) was founded in 1922, but a number of leagues had been in existence prior to that time. In 1967, the NFL merged with another league, the newer and less powerful American Football League (AFL). The newly merged league retained the name National Football League. Today, the NFL has 28 teams split into two conferences, the National Conference (NFC) and the American Conference (AFC). Teams are aligned into three divisions in each conference.

At the end of the regular season, each division champion, plus two **Wild Card** teams (the two other teams with the best records), begin the conference playoffs.

Games are played at the sight of the team with a better record. This is referred to as the **Home Field Advantage**.

AFC	NFC
Eastern Division	***Eastern Division***
Buffalo Bills	Dallas Cowboys
Indianapolis Colts	New York Giants
Miami Dolphins	Philadelphia Eagles
New England Patriots	Phoenix Cardinals
New York Jets	Washington Redskins
Central Division	***Central Division***
Cincinnati Bengals	Chicago Bears
Cleveland Browns	Detroit Lions
Houston Oilers	Green Bay Packers
Pittsburgh Steelers	Minnesota Vikings
	Tampa Bay Buccaneers
Western Division	
Denver Broncos	***Western Division***
Kansas City Chiefs	Atlanta Falcons
Los Angeles Raiders	Los Angeles Rams
San Diego Chargers	New Orleans Saints
Seattle Seahawks	San Francisco 49ers

The Super Bowl

The AFC champion and the NFC champion meet for the NFL championship in the Super Bowl, held in January at a neutral site. The Super Bowl is one of the most hyped sporting events by the media, even though the game itself has developed a reputation as a snoozer.

The Wiffle and the Useful

The two most recent attempts to compete with the NFL for fan support were the World Football League (WFL) and the United States Football League (USFL). The WFL played one full season in 1974 and half of the 1975 year before collapsing with financial problems. The USFL played three full seasons from 1983 to 1985 before it, too, folded. The USFL subsequently filed an antitrust suit against the NFL, won, and was awarded a settlement of $1. Yes, that is one dollar. This was later trebled to an amazing $3.

The Canadian Football League

The CFL has been in existence since 1959 and has gone through various periods of popularity. The Canadian game has several rule differences from the American game, including a longer and wider field, only three downs instead of four, twelve players per side instead of eleven, and a one-point "single" for a punt that goes out of the end zone or a kick that is not returned out of the end zone. Teams in the Canadian League are: British Columbia Lions, Calgary Stampeders, Edmonton Eskimos, Hamilton TigerCats, Ottawa Rough Riders, Saskatchewan Roughriders, Toronto Argonauts, and Winnipeg Blue Bombers.

The World League of American Football

The WLAF was started in 1990 under the direction of the NFL. It is being used to experiment with new rules and to see if expansion into Europe is feasible. The WLAF has teams in Barcelona, Frankfurt, and London in addition to the U.S.

College Football

Most colleges and universities field football teams. They are united by two organizations. The NCAA (National Collegiate Athletic Association) governs the larger schools and the NAIA governs the smaller schools. The NCAA and NAIA are broken up into different divisions for football.

NCAA Division I-A: This is the big time. Schools like Alabama, Texas, and USC are in this category.

NCAA Division I-AA: A step below the big time. Includes schools like Boise State, Georgia Southern, and Yale.

NCAA Division II: This is the lowest level where schools can award athletic scholarships. Members include Portland State (OR), Slippery Rock (PA), and Texas A&I.

NCAA Division III: The lowest level of NCAA play. Includes schools like Ferrum (VA), Hofstra (NY), and St. John's (MN).

NAIA Division I: Roughly equivalent to NCAA Division III, but with even less emphasis. Carson-Newman (TN) and West Virginia Tech are members.

NAIA Division II: Very small schools you probably have never heard of. Unless you're an alumnus of Pacific Lutheran (WA) or Wisconsin-La Crosse.

Most universities at the NCAA Division I-A level (referred to as **Major Colleges**) are members of conferences. A few play independent schedules.

In 1991, a number of major independents—Florida State, Miami, and Penn State—made deals to join established conferences. Other independents then founded the Big East conference for football, leaving Notre Dame as the only major remaining independent.

Big East
Boston College Eagles
Miami Hurricanes
Pittsburgh (Pitt) Panthers
Rutgers Scarlet Knights
Syracuse Orangemen
Temple Owls
Virginia Tech Hokies
West Virginia Mountaineers

Atlantic Coast Conference (ACC)
Clemson Tigers
Duke Blue Devils
Florida State Seminoles
Georgia Tech Yellowjackets
Maryland Terrapins
North Carolina Tarheels
North Carolina State Wolfpack
Virginia Cavaliers
Wake Forest Demon Deacons

Big Ten
Illinois Fighting Illini
Indiana Hoosiers
Iowa Hawkeyes
Michigan Wolverines
Michigan State Spartans
Minnesota Golden Gophers
Northwestern Wildcats
Ohio State Buckeyes
Penn State Nittany Lions
Purdue Boilermakers
Wisconsin Badgers

Southeastern (SEC)
Alabama (Bama) Crimson Tide
Arkansas Razorbacks
Auburn Tigers
Florida Gators
Georgia Bulldogs
Kentucky Wildcats
Louisiana State (LSU) Tigers
Mississippi (Ole Miss) Rebels
Mississippi State Bulldogs
South Carolina Gamecocks
Tennessee Volunteers
Vanderbilt Commodores

Big West
Cal State-Fullerton Titans
Long Beach State 49ers
Nevada-Las Vegas (UNLV) Rebels
New Mexico State Aggies
Pacific Tigers
San Jose State Spartans
Utah State Aggies

Mid-American
Ball State Cardinals
Bowling Green Falcons
Central Michigan Chippewas
Eastern Michigan Hurons
Kent Golden Flashes
Miami of Ohio Redskins
Ohio University Bobcats
Toledo Rockets
Western Michigan Broncos

Pacific Ten (Pac Ten)
Arizona Wildcats
Arizona State Sun Devils
Cal-Berkeley (Cal) Golden Bears
Oregon Ducks
Oregon State Beavers
Stanford Cardinal
UCLA Bruins
USC Trojans
Washington Huskies
Washington State Cougars

Big Eight
Colorado Buffaloes
Iowa State Cyclones
Kansas Jayhawks
Kansas State Wildcats
Missouri Tigers
Nebraska Cornhuskers
Oklahoma Sooners
Oklahoma State Cowboys

Southwest (SWC)
Baylor Bears
Houston Cougars
Rice Owls
Southern Methodist (SMU) Mustangs
Texas Longhorns
Texas A&M Aggies
Texas Christian (TCU) Horned Frogs
Texas Tech Red Raiders

Western Athletic (WAC)
Air Force Falcons
Brigham Young (BYU) Cougars
Colorado State Rams
Fresno State Bulldogs
Hawaii Rainbow Warriors
New Mexico Lobos
San Diego State Aztecs
Texas-El Paso Miners
Utah Utes
Wyoming Cowboys

Major Independent
Notre Dame Fighting Irish

The After Party

Unlike nearly every other sport, major college football (Division I) does not have a playoff system. The other divisions do have playoffs.

Major colleges are ranked by two wire service polls, the AP and *USA Today*. Whoever is #1 in the polls at the end of the year is considered the "**National Champion.**" Only rarely do different teams head each poll at the end of the year. (In 1991, Colorado and Georgia Tech shared the #1 spot.)

The end of the major college football season is marked by a series of **Bowl Games**, which pit the best teams in the nation against each other. Although this is not a playoff system, the bowl games are usually crucial in determining a team's final ranking.

Major Bowl Games	*Less Important Bowl Games*
Fiesta Bowl, Tempe	Blockbuster Bowl, Miami
Orange Bowl, Miami	Freedom Bowl, Anaheim
Rose Bowl, Pasadena	John Hancock Bowl, El Paso
Sugar Bowl, New Orleans	Liberty Bowl, Memphis
Big Bowl Games	*Lame Bowl Games*
Cotton Bowl, Dallas	Aloha Bowl, Honolulu
Florida Citrus Bowl, Orlando	Copper Bowl, Tucson
Gator Bowl, Jacksonville	Independence Bowl, Shreveport
Holiday Bowl, San Diego	Peach Bowl, Atlanta

Also at the end of the year, **The Heisman Trophy** is awarded to the player deemed most outstanding by a nationwide poll of writers. Colleges have taken to publicizing their great players like political candidates, making it increasingly difficult for smaller, less successful football programs to produce an award winner. The award is most often awarded to quarterbacks and running backs, though all players are eligible.

How to Watch a Game

Watching a football game can be exhilarating or sleep-inducing, depending on the teams involved, the style of play, and the company you're with. Besides preparing for the weather, you should be ready to watch for certain things. A long pass is really exciting, as are kickoffs, last-second field goals, interceptions, and blocked punts. Short runs, timeouts, first quarter field goals, and mismatches are surefire snoozers. If you're not completely interested in the game there are a number of things you can do to keep your mind occupied. Decide which team has the better color scheme. Watch the Tiger mascot threaten to eat the yell leader. Make side bets about things that might happen (bet whether they pass or run, or whether a fat offensive lineman will make it off the field in time). Here's a quick etiquette lesson:

When to cheer a little:

1. When a runner gains 10 yards.
2. When a receiver makes a nice catch.
3. When the defense holds the offense on third down.
4. When the band plays at halftime.
5. When the cheerleaders perform.
6. When a drunk guy runs out onto the field.
7. When a player you hate gets replaced.

When to cheer a lot:

1. When a runner gains over 20 yards.
2. When a receiver makes a great catch or scores a touchdown.
3. When the defense intercepts a pass or recovers a fumble.
4. When the band spells out an obscene word.
5. When the USC cheerleaders or the Raiderettes perform.
6. When a drunk girl runs out onto the field.
7. When a player you hate gets ejected.

When to boo:

1. When the concession stand quits selling beer.

Names You Should Know

George Halas: Legendary owner of the Chicago Bears and one of the early founders of the NFL. At one point, he was the owner, coach, and player for the Decatur Staleys (forerunner of the Bears). Called "Papa Bear," Halas coached the Bears from 1922 to 1963.

Tom Landry: Until his recent retirement, he was the only coach the Dallas Cowboys ever had. Responsible for building one of the great pro programs of the '70s. Landry's Cowboys won two Super Bowls.

Vince Lombardi: The archetypical "tough coach" who had a love/hate relationship with his players. Led the Green Bay Packers to the first two Super Bowl titles; in fact, the Super Bowl trophy is named after him. Famous quote: "Winning isn't everything—it's the only thing."

Pete Rozelle: Longtime commissioner of the NFL, Rozelle was partly responsible for making the NFL what it is today. He presided over the most important aspect of the league's growth, the merger of the original NFL with the AFL.

 **Joe Namath**: One of the great "characters" of the game, Namath was a quarterback for the New York Jets. He became a household word in 1969, when he predicted the AFL champion Jets would upset the powerful Baltimore Colts in Super Bowl III. His prediction came true, and "Broadway Joe" began a long string of promotional endorsements and TV appearances.

Al Davis: Team-building genius or sleazy opportunist? Davis is the Managing General Partner of the Los Angeles Raiders who stunned the sports world when he moved the Raiders from their longtime home in Oakland to L.A. Davis never seems to worry about how the public perceives him, sticking instead to his simple philosophy (which has paid off with three Super Bowl titles), "Just win, baby."

Jim Brown: One of the greatest runners to ever play the game, Brown is still remembered for his brute strength and speed. A former football and lacrosse star at Syracuse, Brown led the league in rushing eight times. Only Walter Payton and Tony Dorsett have more total yards.

Red Grange: In many ways he legitimized pro football for the masses. He was such a big star at Illinois that in 1925, the Chicago Bears signed him and went on a fifteen city barnstorming tour. Grange received a percentage of the gate, which turned out to be a substantial amount.

O.J. Simpson: Right up there with Jim Brown as the greatest runner of all time. After an outstanding career at USC, Simpson went on to star for the Buffalo Bills. Though the teams he played for were never that good, Simpson rushed for 11,236 career yards. O.J. is currently a television commentator on NFL games.

Walter Payton: Recently retired from a superb career with the Chicago Bears, Payton is the all-time rushing leader with 16,726. Known as "Sweetness," Payton prided himself on being in better shape than anyone else in the game, and it paid off with a Super Bowl title in 1986.

Don Shula: The second-winningest pro coach of all-time, behind George Halas, Shula coached winning teams at Baltimore and Miami. Considered one of the smartest and classiest coaches in the league, Shula won Super Bowls in 1973 and 1974, and his 1972-73 Dolphin team was 17-0, still an unequaled record.

Joe Montana: Phenomenal quarterback for the San Francisco 49ers who has become the premier quarterback of the current NFL with three Super Bowl titles to his credit. Montana has developed into one of the greatest quarterbacks who has ever played the game, leading the league in a number of categories and specializing in late-game heroics. He is the all-time leader in the passing efficiency category.

Chuck Bednarik: Though you may have never heard of him, Bednarik has the distinction of being the last great two-way player. He starred and was All-Pro at both center and linebacker for the Philadelphia Eagles in the 1950s and early '60s. Amazingly, Bednarik was a key member of Eagle title teams in both 1949 and 1960.

Paul Brown: Coached in the All-America Football Conference from 1946-49 where he won 4 titles before moving on to the NFL. Brown first coached the Cleveland Browns (named after him) to six straight NFL conference titles and three world championships. After that, he moved on to found, coach, and manage the Cincinnati Bengals franchise.

Joe Paterno: Major college football's winningest active coach, Paterno has led Penn State to two national titles.

Paul "Bear" Bryant: A legendary coaching figure who is probably the best-known person in the history of the state of Alabama. His University of Alabama teams were always threats to win national titles. It has been said that no former player of The Bear's would ever say anything bad about him.

Lou Holtz: The bespectacled, inspirational Holtz has restored Notre Dame to championship caliber football since taking over after stints at Arkansas and Minnesota. His Irish won a national championship in 1989 and are in the national title hunt nearly every year.

Great Feats

The Feat: An undefeated NFL season (17-0).
Who Did It: Miami Dolphins.
When and Where: 1972-'73, regular season, playoffs, and Super Bowl.
What Made It Great: It is extremely difficult to go through an NFL season without a loss. The only other teams in history to accomplish this were prior to the modern era.

The Feat: An AFL team winning the Super Bowl: New York Jets 16 Baltimore Colts 7.
Who Did It: The New York Jets.
When and Where: 1969, Miami.
What Made It Great: The AFL was considered (and in most ways was) inferior to the NFL. The first two Super Bowls were blowout victories for the NFL's Green Bay Packers. In this game, brash New York Jets quarterback Joe Namath predicted a Jets win, and, incredibly, fulfilled the promise.

The Feat: A sixty-three yard field goal.
Who Did It: Tom Dempsey, New Orleans Saints.
When and Where: 1970, against Detroit.
What Made It Great: The pudgy, clubfooted Dempsey astonished the football world by making prayer into reality and defeating the Lions with this last-second kick. His feat, from his own thirty seven yard line (the goal posts were placed on the goal line then, rather than 10 yards back as they are today), meant that a team was virtually never out of field goal range. Not long after, the NFL powers that be decided to move the goalposts back 10 yards, and no kick from enemy territory has split the uprights since.

The Feat: 2,003 yards rushing in a single season.
Who Did It: O.J. Simpson.
When and Where: 1973, Buffalo Bills.
What Made It Great: In a fourteen-game season, the former USC college great secured his place in pro and endorsement heaven by reaching a milestone that had been considered unreachable.

Pro Football Fans

The Blue-Collar Guy: Works at one of the city's biggest employers, is very vociferous, and always totes a really big beer. Likes to watch the cheerleaders, but takes the game very seriously, since he paid full freight for his season tickets.

The Corporate Guy: Antithesis of the Blue-Collar Guy, the Corporate Guy is only at the game because his company has free seats. He's dressed more for a Dockers' commercial than for a football game. Cellular phone is always at the ready.

The Hardcore Fan: A walking advertisement for NFL Properties with his team T-shirt, hat, and satin jacket. Has a radio to listen to the game, binoculars, and a program to read statistics aloud to everyone around him.

The Bimbo: Usually has big hair and tight jeans. Often color-coordinated to team colors, but her outfit would never be sanctioned by team officials. Doesn't really like the game, but likes to be seen at events and really likes looking at the huddle.

College Football Fans

The Old Alum: An older gentleman dressed from head to toe in the colors of his school (e.g., bright red for Arkansas). He carries an old pennant from the '50s and sports a big, goofy hat.

The Vanderbilt Preppy: Formal southern guy who wears an oxford cloth shirt and a tie to the games. Sports preppy glasses and has a big plastic cup of beer. Looks like a young George Will.

The Colorado Babe: Looking casually hip with a school sweatshirt and a thoroughly modern haircut, this Colorado coed constantly has a cup of beer in her hand, and knows where the TV camera is.

The S.C. Dude: Falling leaves and topcoats are not part of the Southern Cal football tradition. This guy wears shorts, sunglasses, and a polo shirt, and doesn't really care what the score is.

The Psycho: A temporarily insane member of the student body who paints his face and torso in school colors. Someday he might become a doctor or a lawyer.

Tavern Talk: NFL Arguments

Argument One: Is John Elway a great NFL quarterback or one of the NFL's great disappointments?

+ Elway is a great athlete, able to extricate himself from difficult situations and make spectacular plays out of nothing. His leadership and skills led a mediocre Denver Broncos team to three Super Bowls in four years.

- Elway has a strong arm, but he throws the ball too hard without any touch. He tries to do too much himself, and his less-than-awesome statistics back this up. He is 0 for 3 in the Super Bowl, and the Broncos only got there because the AFC had no tough teams.

Argument Two: Should any franchise be able to move to any city it wants to? If a franchise does move, should the city, rather than the team, retain the old name?

- A franchise belongs to its owners, not to the city. If the owners want to move it to Keokuk, Iowa, they should be able to, just like any other business. Would someone tell Bob's Market that they couldn't move from Kansas City to Wichita? The name of the team (e.g., Cardinals), like the name of a business, should remain with the team, not the city.

+ Certain rules must apply. Al Davis cannot be allowed to move his Raiders to Detroit for example, and usurp the Lions existing fan support. After years in a city, a name like the Colts becomes part of a place like Baltimore. People take pride in the name and treat it as their own. If another franchise is awarded to Baltimore, that franchise should be able to call itself the Colts.

Gridiron Classics

Hollywood has done a fairly decent job of making football films, although hardcore sports nuts would disagree. The key seems to be in limiting the number of football scenes, which are difficult to re-create. But with camera tricks, loud grunting noises, and good music, a number of movies have scored major points with the public. Here are the football flicks that the Sports Literate fan needs to know.

Knute Rockne, All American (1940): Ronald Reagan is Notre Dame back George Gipp, whose early death causes Pat O'Brien, as legendary coach Knute Rockne, to exhort his players to "win one for the Gipper." Walks a fine line between inspiration and hokeyness, much like Reagan's years in the White House.

Paper Lion (1968): A behind-the-scenes look at an NFL training camp, taken from the real-life experience of preppy writer George Plimpton. Alan Alda plays Plimpton, undercover as a rookie QB from Harvard, who gets harassed mercilessly by his Detroit Lions teammates.

Heaven Can Wait (1978): A great cast (Charles Grodin, James Mason, Dyan Cannon) supports Warren Beatty as a pro player who returns from the dead in someone else's body. Great film, with surprisingly effective game shots.

North Dallas Forty (1979): Based on a book by ex-Dallas Cowboy Pete Gent. Nick Nolte is an aging star who begins to realize his time is up and management no longer cares about him. Probably the best football movie ever made, with brutal and violent action scenes.

Everybody's All-American (1987): From a book by star sportswriter Frank Deford. Dennis Quaid is an LSU football legend, and Jessica Lange is his beauty queen wife. A well-made movie that follows Quaid and Lange from the highs of football glory to the lows of middle-aged ennui.

Glossary

Blitz: When one or more linebacker(s) or defensive back(s) rush the quarterback.

Bootleg: A quarterback hides the ball against his leg and runs outside the defense. He can run or pass from this position.

Coffin Corner Kick: A punt aimed to go out of bounds inside the 15-yard line. See *Pooch Kick*.

Dime Defense: When a defense uses two extra defensive backs. See *Nickel Defense*.

Draw Play: When the quarterback looks like he's going to pass, but hands the ball off to a running back.

Flea-Flicker: A trick play, usually one of two things: (1) The quarterback hands to a runner who hands to a receiver who hands back to the quarterback, who throws a pass; (2) The quarterback hands to a runner, who dives into the line, then laterals back to the quarterback, who throws a pass.

Hail Mary: A slang term for a last-second long pass which seems to need some sort of divine intervention in order to succeed.

I-Formation: An offense with two running backs stacked behind the quarterback. See *Pro Set*, *Wishbone*.

Nickel Defense: When a defensive team inserts a fifth defensive back (Get it? Nickel? Five?) Six defensive backs is called, oddly enough, a *Dime*.

Onsides Kick: A short kickoff which the kicking team hopes to recover. It must travel at least ten yards to be considered a legal kick.

Option: A play in which a quarterback has a choice of keeping the ball himself or pitching the ball to a running back. The *Triple*

Option also includes the chance to hand the ball off to another running back.

Pocket: The area behind the offensive linemen, where the quarterback stands to pass. If the defensive pressure is too great, the quarterback can be *"forced out of the pocket."*

Pooch Kick: When a punter taps the ball, trying to make it land inside the 20-yard line. See *Coffin Corner Kick*.

Pro Set: The most common offensive set, with a quarterback, two running backs split behind him, a tight end, and two wide receivers. See *I-Formation, Wishbone*.

Run and Shoot: A wide-open offense featuring four wide receivers and one running back.

Sack: When a defensive player tackles the quarterback for a loss of yards.

Screen: A slow-developing pass play where the quarterback holds on to the ball before throwing it to a back, who is surrounded by a *"screen"* of blockers.

Shank: A very poor punt.

Spike: When a player slams the ball into the ground as a celebration after a touchdown.

Statue of Liberty: An old trick play, rarely seen anymore. The quarterback conceals the ball behind his back, and a receiver comes around behind him, takes it, and runs.

Touchback: This results in the ball coming out to the twenty yard line of the team that just got the ball. It happens when a kick goes out of the end zone or when a player doesn't run the ball out of the end zone after a kick or a turnover.

Wishbone: A college football offense with three backs in the backfield. It is usually predicated on being able to run the *Triple Option*.

Insider Quiz

1. The NFL's "In the grasp" rule:
   - A. Stops play when a defensive player grabs the quarterback.
   - B. Is designed to reduce injuries to quarterbacks.
   - C. Makes a mockery of the game, preventing quarterbacks from making great plays and forcing linemen to ease up.

2. NFL placekickers:
   - A. Are a very important part of a team's offense.
   - B. Often win games in the last second.
   - C. Are wimps.

3. The most important ritual in pro football is:
   - A. Getting taped and padded before the game.
   - B. Spiking the football after a touchdown.
   - C. Dumping Gatorade on the coach after a win.

4. An NFL game:
   - A. Attracts thousands of fans.
   - B. Consists of four 15-minute quarters.
   - C. Lasts twice as long as a Catholic wedding.

5. Army and Navy:
   - A. Used to have powerful football teams.
   - B. Play each other at the end of the year.
   - C. Usually lose to Air Force.

6. USC and Notre Dame:
   - A. Are perennial football dynasties.
   - B. Have played many great games against each other.
   - C. Are universally hated by anyone not from USC or Notre Dame.

7. In the state of Texas, football is:
   - A. A popular sport.
   - B. A very popular sport.
   - C. A religion.

3 Basketball

Basketball

 No sport's origin is as easily traced as is the game of basketball. It began in 1891 in a YMCA in Springfield, Massachusetts. Professor James Naismith, looking for an indoor game to attract more people into the YMCA, had two peach baskets nailed to the balcony of the gymnasium. Players threw a soccer ball into the baskets, and the game was stopped after each "basket" to retrieve the ball. Eventually the bottoms were cut out of the peach baskets (forerunners of today's "hoops") and backboards were added; ironically, the first backboards were not to help shooters but to keep spectators from interfering with shots.

Today's game, while infinitely more developed than Professor Naismith's invention, still retains the basics of his idea: put the round ball through the hoop. Basketball is one of America's "Big Three" sports, along with football and baseball. To be Sports Literate, you will need to know about both college and professional basketball.

Professional Basketball

Professional basketball actually began in the late 1890s, although the National Basketball Association (NBA) didn't start until 1949. That early league was a far cry from the current big-money NBA—it still had teams in places like Sheboygan, Wisconsin, and Waterloo, Iowa. Although it took awhile for pro basketball to catch on, the NBA eventually became one of America's premier sports organizations.

In 1967, a rival league, the American Basketball Association (ABA), sprang up. It was notable for three reasons: (1) It used a red, white, and blue basketball; (2) It introduced the world to Julius "Dr. J" Erving, who would go on to be an NBA superstar; (3) It added four teams to the NBA—in 1976, the ABA was in big financial trouble and worked out a merger deal keeping franchises alive in Denver, Indiana, New York (now New Jersey), and San Antonio.

The NBA currently has 27 teams in two conferences and four divisions, with occasional rotation of the newer teams.

Eastern Conference	Western Conference
Atlantic Division	**Midwest Division**
Boston Celtics	Dallas Mavericks
Miami Heat	Denver Nuggets
New Jersey Nets	Houston Rockets
New York Knicks	Minnesota Timberwolves
Orlando Magic	San Antonio Spurs
Philadelphia 76ers	Utah Jazz
Washington Bullets	
Central Division	**Pacific Division**
Atlanta Hawks	Golden State Warriors
Charlotte Hornets	Los Angeles Clippers
Chicago Bulls	Los Angeles Lakers
Cleveland Cavaliers	Phoenix Suns
Detroit Pistons	Portland Trail Blazers
Indiana Pacers	Sacramento Kings
Milwaukee Bucks	Seattle Supersonics

At the end of the regular season, the champion of each division is given a #1 and #2 seeding in the conference playoffs. The seven remaining teams in each conference fill out the rest of the brackets, and play a best-of-five series in the first round and best-of-seven series after that to determine the conference champions.

The Eastern Conference and Western Conference champions meet in the **NBA Finals**, a best-of-seven-game series for the right to be called the best in the world.

College Basketball

College basketball has seen some ups and downs. It is currently enjoying immense popularity, as evidenced by enormous television contracts and the difficulty in procuring tickets for the college basketball championships.

The college game began to bloom in the 1930s when Ned Irish, the founder of the NBA's New York Knicks, began promoting college games at New York City's Madison Square Garden. Although gambling scandals hurt the game in the '50s, colleges rebounded and have turned their teams into major sports powers.

Like college football, college basketball is governed by two ruling bodies, the NCAA and the NAIA. As in football, the larger schools are members of the NCAA and the smaller schools belong to the NAIA, but more teams play at the NCAA Division I level in basketball. Why? It's much cheaper to maintain a basketball program than a football program, so smaller schools can compete at a higher level.

Again, as in college football, teams generally play as part of conferences or leagues. Most leagues are the same for basketball as for football, although there are some exceptions. For example, some of the best basketball teams in the nation (DePaul, Georgetown, St. John's, Loyola-Marymount) either do not field football teams or have football teams playing in lower divisions.

Conferences Playing Division I Football and Basketball

Atlantic Coast
Big East (Not all members)
Big Eight
Big Ten
Big West (Not all members)
Mid-American
Pac 10
Southeastern
Southwest
Western Athletic

Legendary Coach Phog Allen of Big Eight Kansas

Some Conferences That Play Division I Basketball (But Not Football)

Missouri Valley
Bradley Braves
Creighton Bluejays
Drake Bulldogs
Illinois State Redbirds
Indiana State Sycamores
Southern Illinois Salukis
S.W. Missouri State Bears
Tulsa Golden Hurricane
Wichita State Shockers

Big Sky
Boise State Broncos
Eastern Washington Eagles
Idaho Vandals
Idaho State Bengals
Montana Grizzlies
Montana State Bobcats
Nevada (Reno) Wolfpack
Northern Arizona Lumberjacks
Weber State Wildcats

West Coast Conference
Gonzaga Bulldogs
Loyola Marymount Lions
Pepperdine Waves
Portland Pilots
San Diego Toreros
San Francisco Dons
Santa Clara Broncos
St. Mary's Gaels

**Big East Schools
Playing Division I
Basketball (Not Football)**
Connecticut Huskies
Georgetown Hoyas
Providence Friars
Seton Hall Pirates
St. John's Redmen
Villanova Wildcats

•At the end of the year, sixty-four teams are invited by a selection committee to play in the NCAA tournament.

•The NCAA tournament is a single-elimination tournament played at neutral sites, split into four regions and seeded from strongest to weakest.

•The NCAA tournament semifinal and final games are called the **Final Four** and are played in a different site from any of the tournament games. This is a major national event and is scheduled to be played in huge domed stadiums for years to come (New Orleans Superdome, Indiana Hoosierdome, Seattle Kingdome).

•NIT: This once prestigious post-season tournament now takes NCAA leftovers, and has its "Final Four" in New York City.

How to Watch Basketball

There are two ways to watch basketball. One is to watch every play closely, analyzing the offensive and defensive sets, and criticizing the foolish plays and nodding at the good ones. The other way is to grab a hot dog and a beer, get into the flow of the game, and scream at the great plays and boo at the bad ones.

Most people choose the latter. The great thing about hoops is that it's made to be watched. It offers plenty of action at both ends, enough stoppages of play that you can talk and interact with friends, and players you can see up close without helmets or hats.

It's also a fairly easy game to pick up. Sure there are some weird rules, but if you know the basics, you'll get by. Obviously, the object of the game is to put the orange ball through the orange hoop. Beyond that, you should know about fouls, turnovers, three-point shots, and dunks. You should also learn how to cheer:

Action: Three-point shot.
Reaction: Hold your hands over your head like a touchdown signal.

Action: Turnover or foul by the other team.
Reaction: Point your finger at the guilty player and chant "You! You! You!"

Action: Time-out by the other team when your team is winning.
Reaction: If at game, cheer wildly and look for a TV camera. If at home, cheer wildly and grab another beer.

Action: Dunk.
Reaction: Jump around and high-five your neighbor.

Action: Dunk by a white guy.
Reaction: Look shocked.

Dunk King Michael Jordan

Pro Names You Should Know

Bob Cousy: Probably the best passer to ever play in the NBA. Old highlights of Cousy make Magic Johnson look uncreative. He won six NBA titles playing with the Boston Celtics and led the league in assists eight times.

Wilt Chamberlain: Thought by many to be the greatest to ever play the game, "Wilt the Stilt" or "The Big Dipper" was a seven-footer who played for Philadelphia, San Francisco, and Los Angeles. He once scored 100 points in a game, and averaged 50.4 points per game over an entire season! He won two NBA titles.

Bill Russell: Not as talented as Chamberlain, but playing with a better team, he managed to get the best of Wilt on many occasions. Russell's Boston Celtics won the NBA title an unbelievable eleven times in the thirteen seasons he played. He also was on back-to-back NCAA champion teams at the University of San Francisco.

 **Jerry West**: A great player from West Virginia, who averaged 27 points per game and led the Los Angeles Lakers to one NBA title as a player, and five championships as General Manager. West is known as one of the best shooters of all time.

Oscar Robertson: "The Big O" was a forerunner of today's great NBA athletes. He was in superb physical shape, and averaged over 25 points a game with Cincinnati (now Sacramento) and Milwaukee. Like Bill Russell, Robertson also won back-to-back NCAA titles (at the University of Cincinnati).

Kareem Abdul-Jabbar: Formerly known as Lew Alcindor, Abdul-Jabbar is arguably the best big man to have played the game. After a legendary career at UCLA, he went on to star for the Milwaukee Bucks and the Los Angeles Lakers. With his "sky hook" shot, Abdul-Jabbar averaged over 24 points per game and won six NBA titles in his 20 seasons. He has scored more points than anyone in NBA history (5,762).

Julius Erving: "Dr. J," with his incredible leaping ability, was one of the truly great innovators of the game. He began in the ABA, where he led his teams to two championships, then he became a mainstay of the NBA's Philadelphia 76ers, who won the NBA crown in 1983. Dr. J averaged 28.7 points per game in the ABA and 22 points per game in the NBA, but what he's really remembered for are his soaring slam dunks and his classy personality.

Michael Jordan: "Air Jordan" is the biggest star of the current NBA, who won his first NBA title in 1991. While playing for the Chicago Bulls, Jordan has led the league in scoring five straight years, and only Wilt Chamberlain and Elgin Baylor had higher scoring averages for a season than Jordan's 37.1. King of the endorsements, he's seen daily on TV advertising Nike, Wheaties, Coke, and McDonald's. Jordan's last-minute bank shot won him a national title at the University of North Carolina.

Magic Johnson: Earvin "Magic" Johnson is possibly the most unique basketball player in history. He is a 6'9" point guard who is the best passer since Bob Cousy. He has won three NBA Most Valuable Player awards, and has led the Los Angeles Lakers to five NBA titles. Magic has played all five positions for the Lakers, and usually leads the league in "Triple Doubles" (double figure game statistics in scoring, rebounding, and assists).

Larry Bird: For a period in the 1980's, Bird was the best player in the NBA. His duels with Magic Johnson were spectacular (ironically, in 1979, Johnson's Michigan State team beat Bird's Indiana State in the NCAA final). He led the Celtics to 3 NBA crowns with his no-look passes, his smooth jump shot, and his unselfish team play. Severe injuries have hampered his skills lately, and kept him from performing at his best.

College Names You Should Know

Obviously, there have been thousands of players and coaches who have influenced the game of basketball. While it would be nice to memorize as many of these as possible, you can impress most people with seven names who've had a great impact on college basketball.

John Wooden: The greatest coach in the history of the game. He won more national titles (10) than anyone in college basketball, and his UCLA Bruins dominated the game like no other team ever. He was a demanding coach, but a solid citizen who didn't drink, smoke, or swear. He created a "Pyramid of Success" that has been used by motivators for years. The sight of John Wooden on the bench with his rolled-up program is a sight that will live forever in the eyes of many fans, and certainly numerous opposing coaches.

Pete Maravich: One of college ball's most memorable characters, "Pistol" Pete still holds the record for highest career scoring average in NCAA history at 44.2 points per game. While playing for his father, Press Maravich, at LSU, Pete scored 50 points or more in 28 games, and this was before the 3-point shot. Maravich was an inspiration to thousands of kids with his flashy style of play, his flowing hair, and his droopy socks. He died tragically of a heart attack in 1989 during a pickup game.

Bill Walton: "Big Red" was one of the most dominant players ever to play. At 6'11" he continued the tradition of the dominant UCLA center established by Lew Alcindor. Walton was a free spirit who managed to curtail his beliefs and need for independence to play for the demanding John Wooden. Walton led the Bruins to two NCAA titles before embarking on an NBA career with the Portland Trail Blazers.

Dean Smith: Coach at North Carolina who has won one NCAA title and is known for his classy and solid basketball program. He has coached a number of great players, including James Worthy, Michael Jordan, and Sam Perkins. The new arena at Chapel Hill is named after him (and nicknamed the "DeanDome"). Smith, who led the U.S. Olympic team to a 1976 gold medal, is the winningest active major college coach.

Bobby Knight: Indiana's controversial coach has won three national championships. Many of his peers call him the best coach in America, but he is often criticized because of his temper and his "motivational" methods. He's been known to berate players in public, bench superstars, and start five freshmen. His two most notorious stunts were throwing a chair onto the floor during a game and pulling his team off the floor and into the locker room in a game against the Soviet Union.

John Thompson: An imposing presence at 6'11", Thompson is the coach at Georgetown who took a nothing program and built it into a national power. Along the way, he has been an inspiration and a father figure to a number of black student/ athletes. While some opponents object to the aggressive style of his Hoya teams, Thompson is unmoved by criticism and firmly believes in his system. Thompson has won two NCAA titles.

Jerry Tarkanian: "Tark the Shark" is a classic character who would seem to be more at home in a Martin Scorsese film than a basketball program. His teams at Nevada-Las Vegas often had more talent than NBA expansion teams, but were constantly on the threshold of NCAA probation. Tark is legendary for chewing nervously on a towel during a tight game, stressing aggressive defense and fast-breaking offense, and working with athletes who often have checkered pasts.

Pro Basketball Feats

The Feat: 100 points in a game.
Who Did It: Wilt Chamberlain, Philadelphia Warriors.
When and Where: March 2, 1962, at Hershey, Pennsylvania, in a game against the New York Knicks.
What Made It Great: The next-highest total of all time is 78, also by Chamberlain. He had 59 points in the second half, and was 36 of 63 from the field.

The Feat: 50.4 points per game (and 25.7 rebounds per game) over a season.
Who Did It: Wilt Chamberlain, Philadelphia Warriors.
When and Where: 1961-'62 season.
What Made It Great: Chamberlain has the three highest season scoring averages in history, and five of the top seven. He also has the three highest season rebounding averages in history.

The Feat: Eight NBA titles in a row.
Who Did It: The Boston Celtics.
When and Where: 1958-'59 season to the 1965-'66 season.
What Made It Great: Nowadays it's considered a tremendous feat when a team wins back-to-back NBA titles.

The Feat: 78 consecutive free throws.
Who Did It: Calvin Murphy, Houston Rockets.
When and Where: December 1980-February 1981.
What Made It Great: Murphy didn't miss a free throw in two months, and he ended the year with an all-time high 95.8% free throw percentage.

The Feat: 906 consecutive games played.
Who Did It: Randy Smith, Buffalo/San Diego/Cleveland/New York.
When and Where: February 1972-March 1983.
What Made It Great: In a grueling sport with a high injury factor, Randy Smith did not miss a game in eleven years.

College Basketball Feats

The Feat: Giant-killing upset in an NCAA final.
Who Did It: Villanova University.
When and Where: 1985 in Lexington, Kentucky.
What Made It Great: Georgetown's team was unbelievably powerful, and Rollie Massamino's Villanova team was given little chance even to stay close. Shooting nearly 80% from the field, the Wildcats held on to upset the Hoyas 66-64.

The Feat: Loyola Marymount's Improbable Charge.
Who Did It: Loyola Marymount University.
When and Where: 1989, NCAA Tournament.
What Made It Great: After the tragic death of star center and team leader Hank Gathers, LMU won three straight games over New Mexico State, defending champ Michigan, and Alabama. Only eventual champ Nevada-Las Vegas kept the overachieving Lions from reaching the Final Four.

The Feat: UCLA's 10 Titles in 12 years.
Who Did It: UCLA.
When and Where: 1964 and 1965, 1967-1973, and 1975, NCAA Tournament.
What Made It Great: John Wooden's UCLA Bruins dominated the game like no one ever before or after. Four of those teams went through entire seasons without a loss, including an 88-game victory streak from 1971-'74. Only Texas Western in 1966 and North Carolina State in 1974 broke up the UCLA title string.

The Feat: Inventing the Jump Shot.
Who Did It: Hank Luisetti.
When and Where: 1930's, Stanford University.
What Made It Great: Luisetti totally revolutionized the game with his one-handed shot. Up to that point, players had shot in a relatively awkward two-handed style, but Luisetti's invention soon became the norm.

Pro Basketball Fans

The High-Fiving Guy: Often dressed in a business suit because he came from the office or happy hour, this guy is the epitome of Ameican sports madness. He'll high-five anyone after a big play, and dance in the aisles to old Motown hits.

The Celeb: Since the NBA has become a hot commodity, Hollywood types are grabbing front-row season tickets. Jack Nicholson at Lakers' games is easily the most famous, but nearly every city has its version of the celeb. Often wearing sunglasses, despite the fact that everyone knows who they are, and not averse to leading cheers during a break.

The Babe: Dressed to kill and ready for action. Knows the players' numbers. Knows the players' names. Knows the players' hangouts. Doesn't know you.

Mr. Hard-To-Please: Has had his tickets since the franchise's inception and consistently complains about the current state of the game. He's the first to complain, boo, and head for the parking lot. He's a courtside curmudgeon.

College Basketball Fans

Cameron Crazy: Named after the arena at Duke, their faces are painted blue and white and some wear half a basketball on their heads. They scream, hold up signs, and do some of the cleverest cheers in the history of the game.

Shark Supporter: UNLV fans like their basketball to be like their city, and the result is an arena full of high rollers. The folks are older, they dress better than an average college crowd, but they're just as loud. Sample activity: moving their hands up and down like shark's jaws in honor of Coach Jerry "Tark the Shark" Tarkanian.

Kansas Fanatic: A bit better dressed than the Cameron Crazy, but nearly as wild. Dressed in Jayhawk blue and red, but held back somewhat by Midwestern sensibility. Sample activity: waving hands back and forth over-the-head to symbolize "waving wheat."

Garden Gymrat: A modern day version of the New York kids who used to hang out in Madison Square Garden's early days. Satin jacket with his favorite Big East team, expensive tennis shoes, jeans, and a gold chain plus a whole lot of attitude. Sample activity: hanging out selling or buying a ticket and going crazy when somebody dunks.

Tavern Talk: NBA Trivia

✓Wilt Chamberlain played in 1,045 regular season games and never fouled out.

✓The 1953-54 Baltimore Bullets did not win a game on the road (0-20).

✓Manute Bol is 7'7", grew up in Sudan, averaged nearly 5 blocked shots per game in one season and reputedly killed a lion with his bare hands.

✓The Detroit Pistons beat the Denver Nuggets 186-184 in a triple overtime game in 1983.

✓In 1975, the New Orleans Jazz scored only 20 points in a half vs. Seattle.

✓In the first quarter of a 1987 game against the Los Angeles Lakers, the Sacramento Kings scored 4 points.

✓Only three players played in the ABA from its inception in 1967 to the time of the merger with the NBA in 1976: Byron Beck, Louie Dampier and Freddie Lewis.

✓Some teams from the ABA included (believe it or not): Anaheim Amigos, the Floridians, Memphis Pros, Memphis Sounds, Memphis Tams, Minnesota Muskies, Oakland Oaks, Pittsburgh Condors, Pittsburgh Pipers, Spirits of St. Louis, San Diego Conquistadors and San Diego Sails.

✓The most famous shot in the world is Kareem Abdul-Jabbar's "Sky Hook."

Kareem Abdul-Jabbar's "Sky Hook"

Hoops Classics

Filmmakers have struggled trying
to make a good basketball movie.
Only *Hoosiers* had the right combi-
nation of storyline and hoop realism
to become a classic. Most attempts end up being an ensemble of
actors lamely trying to portray basketball players. Here are five
hoops films which might help you on your journey to Sports
Literacy:

One-on-One (1977): The first legitimate basketball movie.
Written by and starring a young Robby Benson as a hotshot
hooper caught in the hype and pressure of major college basketball. The basketball scenes are pretty good, despite some absurd
shots of Benson going between-the-legs, behind-the-back, and
through a million guys to score a basket.

The Fish That Saved Pittsburgh (1979): Dr. J (Julius Erving),
Harlem Globetrotter Meadowlark Lemon, and Kareem Abdul-
Jabbar show up in this comedy from the disco era about a losing
basketball team that tries astrology to change its luck.

Inside Moves (1980): Not really a basketball film, but an
emotional look at the relationship of an insecure handicapped
man and a volatile, basketball-playing dreamer.

The Great Santini (1980): Not a basketball movie at all, but
includes a phenomenal scene where Robert Duvall goads his
young son into starting a fight in a high school hoop game.

Hoosiers (1985): Based on the true story of a tiny high school
in Indiana that won the state championship against unbelievable odds. Gene Hackman is the coach, Barbara Hershey his
girlfriend, and Dennis Hopper the alcoholic assistant coach. The
basketball scenes are good, but the real strength of this movie is
the re-creation of the atmosphere of high school hoops in a
bygone era.

Glossary

Board: A rebound or to rebound.

Bury the "J": To make a jump shot. See *"J."*

"D": Defense.

Dish: An assist or the act of passing the ball off.

Hack: To foul badly. One who does this is a *Hacker*.

Illegal Defense: When an NBA team plays a zone instead of man-to-man defense.

In the Paint: Inside the foul line or the *Key*.

"J": A jump shot.

NBA Three: A three-point shot from NBA range, which is about three feet further than college range.

"O": Offense.

The Rock: Street slang for the basketball.

See the Floor: To have good peripheral vision.

Skywalk: To jump really high.

Space Eater: A huge guy. Also, an *Aircraft Carrier*.

Swing Man: Someone who can play forward or guard.

Three in the Key: A violation for staying in the key for more than three seconds.

Transition Game: The phase of the game when a team goes from offense to defense and vice versa.

Trey: A three-point shot.

Vitale-Mania

ESPN commentator Dick Vitale has developed a cult following with his unique style of speaking. A number of his phrases have become so popular that they have begun to crop up in everyday basketball vernacular.

1. **P.T.P. or P.T.P.'er:** Prime Time Performer. A clutch player. *"Christian Laettner...he's a P.T.P.'er!"*

2. **P.T.:** Playing time. *"Hey coach, Marcus Lollie wants some P.T!"*

3. **T.O.:** Timeout. *"Get a T.O. Jimmy Boeheim, get a T.O. baby!"*

4. **Beggin' for the rock:** Calling for the ball. *"Look at Montross down on the baseline beggin' for the rock!"*

5. **Rockin' and rollin':** When a home team and its fans are in a groove. *"Rockin' and rollin' here in the Dean Dome...these fans love it!"*

6. **The General:** Indiana basketball coach Bobby Knight. *"It's always tough to come in here and play The General, Robert Montgomery Knight!"*

7. **Trifecta:** (Pronounced "Trifec-ter", derived from horse racing). A three-point shot. *"Harold Miner just pulled up and nailed that trifecta!"*

8. **Diaper Dandy:** An outstanding freshman player. *"I'm tellin' you folks, Damon Bailey is a real diaper dandy!"*

Insider Quiz

1. One thing you'll see on a visit to the University of North Carolina is:
    A. A state-of-the art basketball arena.
    B. Plaques dedicated to former Tarheel greats.
    C. A lot of things colored light blue.

2. An NCAA Final Four appearance brings a college:
    A. Lots of publicity.
    B. Lots and lots of national television exposure.
    C. Lots, lots, and lots of money.

3. As a college basketball referee, you:
    A. Make decent money to watch a game you like.
    B. Show up on television once in a while.
    C. Are hated by men, women, and children.

4. St. John's head coach Louie Carnesecca has:
    A. A great relationship with most of his players.
    B. A fiery bench temperment.
    C. More sweaters than Mr. Rogers.

5. The Utah Jazz got their name:
    A. From team owner Keith Jazz.
    B. After the great jazz music heritage in Salt Lake City.
    C. When the team moved from New Orleans.

6. The best mascot in the NBA is:
    A. The Wheedle, Seattle Supersonics.
    B. The Gorilla, Phoenix Suns.
    C. Jack Nicholson, Los Angeles Lakers.

7. The "Three seconds in the key" rule in the NBA:
    A. Keeps big guys from camping out in the key.
    B. Keeps the offense moving and the defense honest.
    C. Is enforced about once every decade.

4

Baseball

Baseball

 The legend says that General Abner Doubleday laid out the first baseball diamond in Cooperstown, New York, in 1839. Not quite true, but baseball is one of those games that bubbled from the bottom up, where no records were kept and, because everyone seemed to play, no one bothered to write anything down.

It took a bunch of New Yorkers to create a set of rules and challenge another team to a game. That was in 1846 in Hoboken, when the New York Knickerbockers took it on the chin from the New York Nine, 23-1 in four innings. Baseball was born and relief pitchers were already in demand.

Since then, the sport has dealt with scandal, two world wars, player strikes, skyrocketing TV contracts, and outrageous salaries, and stayed alive, even flourished.

The game itself isn't too hard to understand. It's just like softball, only without the keg. But the mystique behind baseball takes some time to learn. Why has "Rotisserie League Baseball" replaced poker night in the homes of anal retentive grown men in most major cities? Why do devotees still still speak of Ty Cobb, Babe Ruth, and Joe DiMaggio in hushed reverence? And why does Hollywood seem to have such a love affair with the national pastime?

Say the word "baseball" to half the top corporate executives in America, and they'll get all wistful and teary and start talking about having a game of catch with their Dad. Don't try to understand it, but if you're going to be Sports Literate, you'll have to realize that in America baseball is more than a sport, it's the soul of sport.

The Teams and Divisions

American League	National League
Eastern Division	***Eastern Division***
Baltimore Orioles	Chicago Cubs
Boston Red Sox	Montreal Expos
Cleveland Indians	New York Mets
Detroit Tigers	Philadelphia Phillies
Milwaukee Brewers	Pittsburgh Pirates
New York Yankees	St. Louis Cardinals
Toronto Blue Jays	
	Western Division
Western Division	Atlanta Braves
California Angels	Cincinnati Reds
Chicago White Sox	Houston Astros
Kansas City Royals	Los Angeles Dodgers
Minnesota Twins	San Diego Padres
Oakland Athletics	San Francisco Giants
Seattle Mariners	
Texas Rangers	•Denver and Miami were added in 1991.

Great Franchise Shifts

1952-'53: *Boston Braves to Milwaukee*. The first major franchise shift took the Braves from their home of 76 years.

1957-'58: *Brooklyn Dodgers to Los Angeles*. The "Bums" headed west for the sunshine and booming population.

1957-'58: *New York Giants to San Francisco*. Following the Dodgers' lead, the Giants left the Big Apple with only one Major League team (before the Mets were created).

1960-'61: *Washington Senators to Minnesota (Twins)*. After 59 years in the nation's capital, the Senators bailed out and moved to the Twin Cities.

1971-'72: *Washington Senators to Texas (Rangers)*. The next Senator franchise also left town, this time for Arlington, a suburb of Dallas.

World Series and Playoffs

Until 1968, choosing the teams for the **World Series** was relatively easy. Each league had eight teams, and the team with the best record in the American League played the team with the best record in the National League.

Occasionally, two teams tied and a playoff was held, one game in the American League, best two out of three in the National. New York Giant Bobby Thompson's famous last inning home run in 1951 beat the Dodgers in the final game of a playoff, capping perhaps the greatest finish in baseball history.

In 1968, expansion teams led to the creation of two divisions within each baseball league, and gave birth to the **League Championship Series**. The series were originally the best three out of five games, but have become best four out of seven (like the World Series) due to the immense revenues they generate for television.

The New York Yankees hold the overall lock on the World Series, having won 22 times in 33 appearances. The lowly Chicago Cubs have gone the longest without a series win, last accomplishing victory in 1908.

The Minors

Unlike basketball and football, baseball developed as a major professional sport before colleges took much interest. In order to develop new young talent, Major League ball clubs established Minor League affiliates in smaller urban areas. Before the advent of television, the Minors provided some small towns with their only exposure to professional sports. As TV grew, however, interest Minor League baseball dwindled. Happily, baby boomers are rediscovering the joys of Minor League baseball, where the game seems a little less commercial, a little more pure.

The Minor Leagues are divided into Rookie Leagues, Class A, AA, and AAA. AAA is one step away from the Majors.

How to Watch a Game

Of all the major sports, baseball may be the easiest to watch, but the hardest to understand. After all, what's difficult about sitting out on a summer night, with a beer and a hot dog and friends and family, watching young men standing around in a field? Every now and then, however, something actually happens, and you'll be expected to give the proper fan reaction.

Home runs are easy, but what about a ground rule double? A pop fly is easy to boo, but what about a sacrifice fly to the warning track? With a little advice, you'll be able to fit in with the best bleacher bum.

When to cheer a little:

1) When a player gets a hit, but the ball doesn't go over the fence.
2) When a fielder makes a good play.
3) When a pitcher strikes out a tough hitter.
4) When the manager kicks dirt on the umpire.
5) When the beer vendor finally gets to your row.
6) When George Steinbrenner finally resigned.

When to cheer a lot:

1) When the ball goes over the fence on the fly.
2) When a really fast runner steals a base.
3) When a pitcher goes all nine innings without giving up a hit.
4) When a wild pitch hits an umpire below the belt.
5) When a fellow fan disrobes.
6) When Jose Canseco strikes out.

When to boo:

1) When a great-looking person sitting next to you is booing.

Tavern Talk: Things to Hate

There's plenty to hate about baseball, but the Sports Literate fan confines his targets to things he can do nothing about. You'll never catch an authentic fan grumbling about the amount of gristle in his Polish sausage, or the high cost of parking. Instead, you'll see him complaining about night baseball ("The game was meant to be played during the day") or the salaries of players ("What do they care, they still get their million even if they get hurt").

Some things which may seem obvious to hate—the tendency for a game to become deathly dull, the sad attempt to convince fans that some managers actually have a strategy, and the fact that the "tale of the tape" home run measurements are just made up by some guy in the press box—are off limits: to be Baseball Literate, you'll need to learn what to hate and what not to hate.

Do Hate:
- A particular player, umpire, or owner
- Modern ballparks
- Television's increasing influence
- Any announcer but Harry Caray and Jack Buck
- The Designated Hitter rule
- The A's
- The New York *Times* Sports section
- George Will
- Ground rule doubles

Don't Hate:
- All players, umpires, or owners
- Old, rickety anachronisms, like Tiger Stadium
- Your favorite team being on TV every night
- Harry Caray and Jack Buck
- The fact that pitchers hit unbelievably poorly
- The Cubs
- *USA Today's* Sports section
- Jim Bouton
- Inside the park home runs

Names You Should Know

No game creates more discussion of great players and their feats than baseball. Who was better? Ty or the Babe? Was Aaron's record as great as Ruth's? Aaron had more games (162) per year than Ruth (154), and Ruth was a pitcher for six years. So, wasn't Ruth better? No one knows the answers to arguments about baseball legends. But next time you hear one, you can bet it will involve one or more of the following:

Ty Cobb: His record for the highest lifetime batting average will never be broken, and his records for most hits (broken by Pete Rose) and stolen bases (broken by Lou Brock and Rickey Henderson) stood for over 50 years. Irascible, ornery, sometimes mean, Cobb could cut a shortstop raw with his sharpened spikes while stealing a base, then smile the biggest smile in the world.

Shoeless Joe Jackson: Baseball's great tragic character. One of the greatest natural hitters of all time, whose lifetime batting average (.356) is second only to Cobb's in the American League, he was banned from baseball for life after allegedly taking part in the plot to throw the 1917 World Series. He was excluded from the Hall of Fame, despite the fact that he hit nearly .400 during the Series.

Babe Ruth: Though Hank Aaron hit more home runs in a career, and Roger Maris hit more in a season, no one revolutionized the game like Babe Ruth. In an era where eight or nine home runs a year were enough to lead the league, The Babe was the first to hit thirty, then fifty, then sixty. He was a bigger than life character who rose from a Baltimore orphanage to become the most visible baseball player of all-time. Ironically, he came up as a pitcher, and his record of scoreless World Series innings stood for 42 years. His gregarious personality gave fans a more approachable hero than Cobb's studied dank demeanor.

Joe DiMaggio: Perhaps the most loved player of all. Before he was Mr. Coffee, Joe DiMaggio was Mr. Clutch, coming through with hits or great fielding plays, helping the Yankees to victory, so effortlessly. By hitting safely in 56 consecutive games in 1941, he etched a record into the books which might last forever.

Ted Williams: The Splendid Splinter, contemporary and sometime nemesis of DiMaggio, Williams nearly always hit for a higher average, but DiMaggio nearly always went to the World Series. Williams was the John McEnroe of his day— a bad boy perfectionist who was never quite satisfied and always one bad call away from a tantrum. But he may be the last man to ever hit over .400.

Jackie Robinson: The man who broke the color barrier by joining the Brooklyn Dodgers in 1947. More than just a good player, Robinson needed to be a statesman. He played gracefully under pressure and opened the sport up for generations of great black athletes.

Willie Mays: A great baseball player needs to do five things well: run, throw, field, hit, and hit for power. Willie Mays combined these skills better than perhaps any player ever. He was the most exciting player since Babe Ruth, and ushered in the era of the superstar.

Hank Aaron: Henry Aaron proved that slow and steady wins the race by breaking Babe Ruth's record though he never hit more than 45 home runs in a season. An all-around player with just the right skills to break the record they said would never be broken: Ruth's 714 home runs. Hammerin' Hank finished with 755 homers.

Connie Mack: Mr. Mack, as the players knew him, managed the Philadelphia Athletics for fifty years. He always wore suits in the dugout, which made him look more like a banker than a manager. He could be bold: in 1915, he traded his entire infield because they were making too much money (a combined $100,000).

Casey Stengel: New York Yankees manager during the wildly successful years of the 1950s and '60s with Mickey Mantle, Roger Maris, and Yogi Berra. Famous for "Stengelese," his rambling approach to the English language that broke up a congressional committee with laughter when he was a witness to a panel analyzing baseball's monopoly.

Billy Martin: A comic/tragic character, Martin managed several teams to divisional titles. His vitriolic feuds with Yankee owner George Steinbrenner, as well as random fights with fellow bar-goers, will go down in baseball history. Steinbrenner hired and fired Martin as Yankee manager five times from 1975 to 1988. He died in a car wreck in 1989 at age 61.

Judge Kennesaw Mountain Landis: The first and most famous baseball commisioner, appointed by the owners in the wake of the 1919 "Black Sox" World Series scandal (when a gambling ring tried to fix the World Series). The owners chose Landis, a former federal judge, to adjudicate the case against the Chicago White Sox players, and he began his long career with a bang, by banning eight men on the team from the game of baseball for life.

Bill Veeck: The peg-legged Wizard of Marketing, Veeck kept baseball fun for fans in the Midwest for more than fifty years. With the St. Louis Browns in the 1940s, he brought a midget to the plate to draw a famous four-pitch walk. Thirty years later, he put shorts on his Chicago White Sox players. Funny, charming, and always enthusiastic, Veeck never forgot that baseball was a game for kids.

George Steinbrenner: For seventeen years, Steinbrenner was the epitome of a meddling front office ninny. As owner of the New York Yankees in the '70s and '80s, he was brash and outspoken, with a big ego and checkbook. He started legendary feuds with players and managers like Reggie Jackson and Billy Martin. In 1990, he was removed from his right to direct the team by commissioner Fay Vincent, for indiscretions.

Lou Gehrig: The greatest first baseman ever, and holder of a record as unbreakable as DiMaggio's: 2,130 consecutive games played. "The Iron Horse" was a key member of the great New York Yankee teams in the '20s and '30s, and had a lifetime batting average of .340. He died tragically of amyotrophic lateral sclerosis, which from then on was known as "Lou Gehrig's Disease."

Pete Rose: "Charlie Hustle," the man who for so many years epitomized the hard-nosed ball player, was banned from the game in 1989 for associating with gamblers and betting on his own team. This may keep him out of the Hall of Fame, but cannot blemish his accomplishments, including having the most ever lifetime hits (4,256).

Nolan Ryan: Baseball's all-time strike out leader and pitcher of an unbelievable seven no-hitters, Ryan has a blazing fastball that still serves him well at age 44.

Bo Jackson: A remarkable athlete who plays both pro football and pro baseball. The highlight of his baseball career came in 1989, when he was MVP of the All Star Game. A serious football injury, however, threatens to cut his career short.

Jose Canseco: Love him or hate him, Canseco has become the most visible player in the modern game. He became the first player in history to steal 40 bases and hit 40 home runs in a season, but he is just as famous for his off-field skirmishes with the press and the law.

Great Names to Name Drop

James (Cool Papa) Bell
Mordecai (3-Finger) Brown
Charlie (Jolly Cholly) Grimm
Sal (The Barber) Maglie
Walter (Rabbit) Maranville

Johnny (Pepper) Martin
Harold (Pie) Traynor
Lloyd (Little Poison) Waner
Paul (Big Poison) Waner
Joe (Smoky Joe) Wood

Great Feats

The Feat: Hitting safely in 56 consecutive games.
Who Did It: Joe DiMaggio, New York Yankees.
When: 1941.
What Made It Great: With so many ways to make an out in baseball, with increased travel, night baseball, better relief pitching, DiMaggio's feat required superhuman consistency, concentration, and luck. Only two players have come within 12 games of the record by hitting in 44 straight: Wee Willie Keeler in 1897, and Pete Rose in 1978.

The Feat: The last man to bat over .400 in a season.
Who Did It: Ted Williams, Boston Red Sox.
When: 1941.
What Made It Great: That's right, the same year that DiMaggio stupefied the baseball world with his streak, Old Teddy Ballgame was busy breaking the .400 barrier, a region that George Brett nearly invaded in 1980 (when he hit .390), and Rod Carew in 1977 (at .388), but no one else has dared disturb. It's been fifty years, and besides Brett and Carew, only one other player has come close. One man hit .388 in 1957 and might have passed the mark if his nearly 40-year-old legs had been younger and allowed him to beat out just six more hits. Who was he? Ted Williams.

The Feat: 24 consecutive pitching victories.
Who Did It: Carl Hubbell, New York Giants.
When: 1936-'37.
What Made It Great: The famous screwball pitcher who made his name by striking out five of the game's greatest sluggers in the 1934 All-Star Game (Ruth, Gehrig, Foxx, Simmons, and Cronin). He showed consistency and tenacity in an era of great hitters, breaking the record of 19 straight victories set by Rube Marquard of the Giants in 1912.

The Feat: A perfect no-hit game in a World Series.
Who Did It: Don Larsen, New York Yankees.
When: October 8, 1956 against the Brooklyn Dodgers.
What Made It Great: Only the seventh perfect game in the history of baseball, thrown at the World Series against supposedly one of the two best teams in the game.

The Feat: Two consecutive no-hit games.
Who Did It: Johnny Vander Meer, Cincinnati Reds.
When: June 11 and June 15, 1938.
What Made It Great: The odds of throwing a no-hitter are 1 in 2,000. The odds of throwing two in a career are 1 in 6,000. The odds of throwing two in *a row* are 1 in 100,000.

The Feat: 14 pennants in 16 years, with 9 World Series championships, including 5 in a row.
Who Did It: The New York Yankees under Casey Stengel (and Ralph Houk).
When: 1949-'63.
What Made It Great: These were the "Damn Yankees," when New York City was the center of the world, the years of DiMaggio and Mantle. Today, in the era of free agency, the cost of keeping such a core team together would be prohibitive.

The Feat: 61 home runs, season.
Who Did It: Roger Maris, New York Yankees.
When: 1961.
What Made It Great: The most home runs ever hit in one season. True, the American League schedule had eight more games than it did in 1927 when Ruth hit 60, but with night games, better relief pitching and rougher travel schedules, the feat was monumental. Ironically, Maris' feat has now lasted almost as long as Ruth's did; no player has hit more than 52 home runs since.

The Feat: Pitching seven no-hit games, career.
Who Did It: Nolan Ryan, various teams.
When: 1969-91.
What Made It Great: Only one other pitcher (Sandy Koufax) threw half as many. No-hit games number six and seven came when Ryan was 43 and 44 years old. He's the greatest strikeout artist in the history of the game.

Baseball Fans

The Cute Little Kid: They say baseball brings out the little kid in all of us, so it's great to see a little tyke tag behind his Mom and Dad to the Grand Old Game. It's great to see the young fan full of hope as he waits for his favorite star to sign an autograph. And it's especially great to see the little guy peddle his newfound treasure to an overgrown adolescent psychotic at a baseball card show.

The Giggly Couple: He points out what an "error" means, and she laughs. She kisses his nose, and he titters. They buy the program and keep score for an inning or two, until they start to tickle each other. Best bet: move a seat or two away.

The Screamer: Watch out for this guy. He spends the whole day at the office in a bland job with little human contact, so he gets in his quota at the ballpark. He usually picks out one player who he hates for some weird reason ("I don't like the way he wears his hat") and he goes after him with a vengeance. Favorite lines: "You suck!" "Your mother sucks!" "Hey—you suck!" "Hey—your mother sucks!"

The Frat Guys: They may actually be frat guys, or they may be young professionals adhering to the Frat Axiom ("Whenever four or more men gather in one place, beer will appear and they will become frat guys"), but the net result is the same: lots of incoherent yelling, lots of beer drinking, occasional obscenities, and a probable fight.

Diamond Classics

This has been by far the most successful medium for Hollywood filmmak-
ers. There is a solid baseball film tradition going back to the
1930s and it has continued up through the '90s. Most baseball
movies are well shot, realistic, and true to the game. Even the
comedies have captured the spirit of baseball without looking
idiotic. Here's a list of some great and not-so-great films that
may help you become Baseball Literate.

The Pride of the Yankees (1942): Gary Cooper plays Lou
Gehrig as an earnest and forthright Mama's boy who proves his
mettle by not missing a game for more than fourteen years.

Bang the Drum Slowly (1973): Michael Moriarty, Robert
DeNiro. Kinda' sappy, but a pretty good look at the ups and
downs of minor league life.

The Natural (1984): Robert Redford, Glenn Close. Adapted by
Barry Levinson from Bernard Malamud's novel. Ballplayers as
knights, women as seductresses, and lights as fireworks.

Bull Durham (1988): Kevin Costner, Susan Sarandon. The
best baseball movie at depicting the flavor of the game and the
peculiar mindset of ballplayers.

Eight Men Out (1988): Charlie Sheen, John Cusack. Almost
a documentary look at how members of the 1919 Chicago White
Sox threw their lot in with a nefarious group of gamblers and
paid the ultimate price.

Major League (1989): Charlie Sheen, Corbin Bernsen. Those
wacky Cleveland Indians and their ensuing zany antics.

Field of Dreams (1989): Kevin Costner, Amy Madigan. A
lyrical look at how baseball, myth, and manhood intertwine in
the American psyche.

Glossary

Balk: Once the pitcher stands on the pitching rubber and moves toward the hitter, he must throw the ball toward the plate. If he fails to throw, or tries to pick off a runner on a base, it's a balk and any base runners advance one base.

Clean-up Hitter: The fourth batter in the line-up, so called because, if the first three hitters get on to load up the bases, he would "clean up" with a hit. Generally the most powerful hitter on the team.

Double Play: When two players are put out on the same hit ball, usually a ground ball to the infield.

Double Steal: Usually with a runner at first and second and less than two out. Both runners head for the next base, with the lead runner hoping to beat the catcher's throw and the second runner sneaking in while no one is looking.

Ground Rule Double: When the ball bounces in fair territory and goes over the fence on one hop, the batter and any base runners are entitled to two bases.

Hit and Run: A base stealing ploy whereby the runner on first takes off as a ball is pitched, and the batter tries to hit the ball to right field. The runner then has the chance to get to third rather than stopping at second.

In the hole: Up after the on-deck hitter.

Inside-the-Park Home Run: Occasionally, a ball gets so completely through the defenses that a speedster can make it around the bases before the throw can greet him at home plate. He's rewarded with a home run, just as statistically potent as a stratosphere shot by the Babe.

On Deck: Up next.

Perfect Game: A pitcher keeps all batters from reaching base.

Pick-off Move: When a pitcher throws over to first or wheels around to throw to second instead of pitching to the batter. Rarely successful in catching the runner off base, the pick-off move is just one more element in the cat-and-mouse game on the basepaths.

Rotisserie League Baseball: Bizarre, almost Druidian baseball game created by groups of men in major cities. They buy and trade players and base standings on real performance of the player in the majors. Sort of like Dungeons and Dragons for baseball freaks.

Spitball: A baseball covered with saliva, Vaseline, or water, which makes the ball move wildly. The pitch has been outlawed since the 1920s, but is still supposedly practiced by some unscrupulous and unsanitary zealots.

Strike Zone: Area between the armpits and the knees of the batter in which the pitcher must throw the ball for it to be counted as a strike. Baseball pundits maintain that the National League umpires call lower strikes, and American umps call higher ones.

Suicide Squeeze: Rarely attempted, but occasionally seen in a close game with very little hitting. With a man on third, the batter squares around to bunt while the runner races home. If the bunt is successful, run scores, game over. If the batter misses, runner out, game all but over.

Texas Leaguer: A bloop hit which drops between the infield and outfield.

Triple Play: When three offensive players are put out on the same hit ball. One of the rarest and most exciting plays in baseball. The *unassisted triple play* is the rarest form of all.

Turning Two: Successfully executing a double play.

Warning Track: Dirt along the outfield fence which warns outfielders of the impending fence.

Insider Quiz

1. The most important player in baseball is:
    A. The shortstop.
    B. The late-inning reliever.
    C. The agent.

2. The rarest sight at a baseball game is:
    A. The triple play.
    B. The inside-the-park home run.
    C. A batter not grabbing his crotch.

3. The difference between a superstar and an ordinary player is:
    A. A great arm.
    B. The ability to hit in the clutch.
    C. A paternity suit.

4. The job of the ballgirl is:
    A. To sweep off the bases.
    B. To keep stray foul balls from injuring fans.
    C. To wait for *Playboy* to do a "Girls of the Big Leagues" pictorial.

5. When do you see the best swings in baseball?
    A. During batting practice.
    B. When the game is on the line.
    C. During a bench-clearing brawl.

6. The most important equipment in a major league baseball game is:
    A. The glove.
    B. Spikes.
    C. Diamondvision.

7. These factors could cause a baseball game to be played at a different time:
    A. Rain.
    B. An earthquake.
    C. The Nielsen ratings.

5

Hockey & Soccer

Ice Hockey

 Ice hockey is a fast-paced game that people seem to love or hate. In some areas of the world, it's *the* sport, the king of the hill. In other areas, it's unheard of. From a spectator's standpoint, a hockey game can be incredibly interesting to watch in person, but often a bore on television. Part of the problem with hockey on TV is that cameras cannot do justice to the speed of the game or the fact that the players are doing amazing athletic feats on skates.

Canada is usually considered the birthplace of hockey, and it remains the most popular sport in that country. Although still debated, the origins of ice hockey most likely lie somewhere in eastern Canada in the late 1800s, with some people playing on a frozen pond with a ball and some sticks. Other stories claim that the game is a winter version of field hockey or developed from a French game called "hoquet," played by shepherds. Aliens are another possible source of the origins of the game. Whatever the case, the professional game as we know it today was developed in Canada, and to a lesser extent, the United States.

While some high schools and many colleges play ice hockey, fan support is highest for the professional game. Even foreign nations (the Soviet Union, Czechoslovakia, Finland, and Sweden are the best foreign teams) are considered professionals, despite their long-standing participation in amateur events. The first ice hockey league was developed in Kingston, Ontario, in 1885. In 1893 the **Stanley Cup** (named after Canada's Governor General, Lord Stanley) was awarded to Montreal as the best hockey team in Canada. Real professional teams came on the scene in the 1900s, and the Stanley Cup became a Western vs. Eastern competition, with the Pacific League champ playing the Eastern League winner.

Professional Hockey

The National Hockey League (NHL) was formed in 1926, and soon became the only major ice hockey league in North America. From 1942 to 1967, the NHL consisted of six teams, two in Canada (Montreal and Toronto) and four in the U.S. (Boston, Chicago, Detroit, and New York). Today's NHL consists of twenty-one teams split into two conferences and four divisions. The Stanley Cup is still the trophy awarded to the champion of the league.

Wales Conference

Adams Division
Boston Bruins
Buffalo Sabres
Hartford Whalers
Montreal Canadiens
Quebec Nordiques

Patrick Division
New Jersey Devils
New York Islanders
New York Rangers
Philadelphia Flyers
Pittsburgh Penguins
Washington Capitals

Campbell Conference

Norris Division
Chicago Black Hawks
Detroit Red Wings
Minnesota North Stars
St. Louis Blues
Toronto Maple Leafs

Smythe Division
Calgary Flames
Edmonton Oilers
Los Angeles Kings
Vancouver Canucks
Winnipeg Jets

In 1990, three new franchises were awarded: San Jose Sharks, Ottawa Senators, and Tampa Bay Lightning. San Jose joins in 1991, the others in 1992. They will be placed temporarily in divisions until realignment discussions are completed.

The World Hockey Association (WHA)

This was a short-lived competitor to the NHL, which began in the 1972-'73 season and lasted seven years. Upon its demise, the NHL absorbed four teams from the WHA: Edmonton, Hartford, Quebec and Winnipeg.

How to Watch Hockey

Ice Hockey is one of the world's best games for the true fan. There's fast and furious action, great shooting and stick handling, and rough-and-tumble play.

Hockey for the novice, on the other hand, can seem like nothing more than a bunch of Canadians chasing a tiny rubber thing with long sticks and randomly slugging the hell out of each other. There are two ways to learn to enjoy watching hockey. One is to move to Canada. If that's not appealing, then memorize the following rules. They're easy to learn, and much more exciting than living in Winnipeg.

1. The game is played on an ice hockey "rink" and, obviously, the players wear ice skates. These skates do not have jagged edges at the tip of their blades, like the kind Brian Boitano wears.

2. The game is played with a hard rubber disk called a "puck." Never call the puck the "ball."

3. The object of the game is to put the puck past the goalie and into the net for a "goal." Goals are scored much less frequently than baskets in basketball. A combined total of 3-6 goals is about average. 6-8 goals is a lot. More than 8 means the defense sucks.

4. Most of the players are Canadians. There are some Americans and some Europeans, but Canada remains the leading supplier of talent to the professional hockey leagues.

5. Hockey fights, unlike those in pro wrestling, are real. In fact, hockey players often have false teeth.

6. The lower the skill of a player, the better a fighter he is.

7. Nobody fights with The Great One, even though they could take him easily.

8. The Great One is Wayne Gretzky (See next page.)

Names You Should Know

If you're a diehard hockey fan, these names may seem like repeating the alphabet, but if you're trying to become Sports Literate, they're essential. Luckily for the uninitiated, a little knowledge of a few hockey names can go a long way.

Wayne Gretzky: Called "The Great Gretzky" or "The Great One," Gretzky is that rare athlete most people see once or twice in a lifetime. He is the best-known hockey player of all time, and possibly the most dominant athlete of the modern era of sports. He has scored more points than anyone in the history of the game and was part of four Stanley Cup championships in five years at Edmonton. It was a day of mourning in Canada when the Oilers traded Gretzky to the Los Angeles Kings.

Mario Lemieux: He was on target to break some of Gretzky's scoring records until a back injury put his record-setting in jeopardy. A phenomenal skater and stick-handler, Lemieux led the Pittsburgh Penguins from obscurity to a Stanley Cup title in 1991. He is the only current player who is even mentioned in the same breath with Gretzky.

Bobby Hull: A legendary goal scorer for the Chicago Black Hawks, Hull won the NHL scoring title three times and was league MVP once. Hull's son Brett is now a prolific goal-scorer with the St. Louis Blues.

Gordie Howe: A great all-around player who played an amazing 26 seasons, Howe led the league in scoring five times and was a five-time MVP. Only Wayne Gretzky has scored more points than Howe, who was a first-team All-Star pick ten times.

Bobby Orr: Orr was the best defenseman to ever play the game. He was a mainstay of a Boston Bruins team that won two Stanley Cups. Orr was the league MVP three times and won the Norris Trophy for best defenseman an unbelievable eight years in a row.

Tavern Talk: Hockey Facts

The NHL is clearly a league of dynasties. Consider the following statistics:

✓In an eight-year period (1976-83) only two teams won the Stanley Cup (Montreal and the New York Islanders).

✓In a thirteen-year period (1976-88) only three teams won the Stanley Cup (Montreal, the Islanders, and Edmonton).

✓In a fifteen-year period (1974-88) only four teams won it (Montreal, the Islanders, Edmonton, and Philadelphia).

✓Only once in a seven-year period (1984-1990) did the Stanley Cup leave the province of Alberta (Montreal in 1986).

The Dynasties
1974: Philadelphia Flyers
1975: Philadelphia Flyers
1976: Montreal Canadiens
1977: Montreal Canadiens
1978: Montreal Canadiens
1979: Montreal Canadiens
1980: New York Islanders
1981: New York Islanders
1982: New York Islanders
1983: New York Islanders
1984: Edmonton Oilers
1985: Edmonton Oilers
1986: Montreal Canadiens
1987: Edmonton Oilers
1988: Edmonton Oilers
1989: Calgary Flames
1990: Edmonton Oilers

Glossary

Assist: Given to the one (or two) players who touch the puck last before a third player scores.

Blue Line: A line on the ice which serves as the offsides line.

Center: As a noun, it's a player who stays in the middle of the ice. As a verb, it means to send a puck toward the middle of the ice.

Check: To block an opponent into the boards or onto the ice.

Crease: The square area surrounding a goalie's net. No player but the goalie is allowed to stand inside it.

Face-off: Like a jump ball in basketball, the referee drops the puck between two players to start play.

Glove Save / Stick Save: A *glove save* is when the goalie catches the puck in his glove. A *stick save* is when he turns a shot away with his stick.

Hat Trick: When a player score three goals in a game.

High Sticking: A penalty. It occurs when a player raises his stick above his torso, or menaces another player with an upraised stick.

Offsides: The player with the puck must precede all other offensive players across the blue line.

Penalty Box: An area where players are sent if they are called for a penalty. Minor penalties are two minutes, major penalties are five or ten minutes.

Penalty Shot: A special one-on-one situation between a shooter and a goalie. This is awarded by the referee when a player with a clear breakaway is pulled down intentionally.

Power Play / Short-handed: When players are sent to the penalty box, it is possible that one team may have more players than another. The team with more is said to be on a *power play*, while the team with fewer is said to be *short- handed*.

Puck: The hard rubber disk that is hockey's "ball."

Pulling the Goalie: When a team is losing late in the game, they may elect to take their goalie out of the game, and replace him with another attacking skater. The risk, of course, is that the goal remains unprotected.

Slap Shot: When a player winds up and wallops the puck for a hard shot on goal. Some slap shots have been clocked in excess of 100 mph.

Hockey Awards

Stanley Cup: A huge silver trophy awarded to the champion of the NHL.

Hart Trophy: Given to the most valuable player in the league.

Ross Trophy: Won by the NHL scoring champion.

Calder Memorial Trophy: Rookie of the year.

Lady Byng Memorial Trophy: Given to a player who most epitomizes sportsmanship and gentlemanly conduct.

Vezina Trophy: (Pronounced VEZ-ih-nah). Awarded to the goalie with the best goals-against-average.

Norris Memorial Trophy: Given to the best defenseman in the league.

Conn Smythe Trophy: Won by the MVP of the Stanley Cup playoffs.

Soccer

 Soccer (called "football" outside of America) is the most popular sport in the world, an indelible part of the everyday culture of almost every nation. Unfortunately, the game has one big problem: it has never caught on in the United States.

Soccer, in fact, is somewhat of a second-class citizen in the U.S. Sports fans tend to look down on it as less than manly. There is, however, a small but loyal group of fans who support soccer in a number of different forms.

Amateur Soccer: High school and college soccer are big in certain areas. St. Louis is the nation's hotbed, where Anheuser-Busch has donated equipment and sponsored teams, leagues, and even fields. Perennial collegiate soccer powers include Indiana, UCLA, Rutgers, St. Louis, and Virginia.

Professional Soccer: Outdoor pro soccer has gone through different stages of popularity in the US. In the '70s, the North American Soccer League (NASL) drew some very large crowds, mainly with the help of older foreign stars like Pele, Giorgio Chinaglia, and Franz Beckenbauer. Currently, American professional soccer is in a down period, with little activity beyond certain local leagues.

Indoor Soccer: The Major Indoor Soccer League (MISL) is extremely popular, but only in selected markets like Kansas City, Baltimore, Wichita, and Cleveland. The indoor game is faster than the outdoor game. Caroms off the boards add a hockey-like element, and the scores are often quite high.

International Soccer: Many Americans, particularly those with roots in foreign countries, follow the overseas professional leagues. The most popular leagues are the English and Scottish leagues, the German "Bundes" league, and the Italian league. Scores are usually available in larger daily papers one day a week or in a soccer magazine.

Essential Soccer Knowledge

The World Cup: This is soccer's World Series/Super Bowl/ Royal Wedding. It happens once every four years and alternates between a North or South American site and one in Europe. Nations must qualify through preliminary rounds. The United States, unbelievably, qualified for the Cup in 1990, and because it is the host nation in 1994, received an automatic qualifying berth. American marketers now have to struggle to make the World Cup hot, or risk exposing American soccer malaise to the world more prominently than ever.

The World's Best: The best soccer playing nations usually include: Argentina, Brazil, England, Germany, Italy, the Netherlands, and the Soviet Union.

Hooliganism: British soccer fans are notorious for their violent antics. "Hooligans" follow their teams from town to town and even nation to nation, causing trouble for both opposing fans and the authorities.

Eight Popular British Teams	**Eight World Famous Players**
Arsenal Crystal Palace Liverpool Manchester United Nottingham Forest Queen's Park Rangers Tottenham Hotspur West Ham	Pele (Brazil) Maradona (Argentina) Paolo Rossi (Italy) Peter Shilton (England) Johan Cruyff (Holland) Zico (Brazil) George Best (N. Ireland) Franz Beckenbauer (Germany)

Insider Quiz

1. A famous comedian's joke about hockey is "I went to a fight and..."
   - A. "...scored a goal."
   - B. "...I saw Mario Lemieux there."
   - C. "...a hockey game broke out."

2. In hockey, the Zamboni is:
   - A. When a player does a 360 turn before shooting the puck.
   - B. A special curved stick.
   - C. The machine that cleans and smooths the ice between periods.

3. A bad day in Canada is:
   - A. When a Canadian team loses to an American team.
   - B. A blackout during "Hockey Night in Canada."
   - C. Both of the above, plus a beer strike.

4. In hockey, the best example of "an exercise in futility" is:
   - A. Trying to check The Great Gretzky.
   - B. Trying to stop a penalty shot.
   - C. Rooting for the Vancouver Canucks.

5. Indoor soccer's unofficial marketing slogan is:
   - A. "The world's best, playing under a roof."
   - B. "The fastest game in the world."
   - C. "These guys look great in shorts."

6. Americans should be happy if the U.S. World Cup team:
   - A. Wins the World Cup.
   - B. Wins a game.
   - C. Scores a goal or two.

7. The most important thing to take to a British soccer match is:
   - A. An umbrella.
   - B. A scarf with team colors.
   - C. A sharpened screwdriver to fight your way out of the stadium.

6
Golf

Golf

 Historians believe golf began in Scotland during the 1440s. By 1457, the game's popularity became so widespread that Scotsmen were foregoing traditional archery practice in favor of an afternoon on the golf links. This trend concerned the Scottish Parliament (since good archers were essential in the frequent battles Scotland waged against England), and the game was prohibited until 1491.

The game's first official championship was held in 1861 when Scotland's Prestwick Golf Club sponsored a tournament that wasn't just for its members, but rather "open to the world." Thus, the British Open was born.

Golf in America began around 1888 when a group of Scotsmen established the St. Andrews Golf Club of Yonkers, New York. The U.S. Open championship began soon after and the game grew steadily in popularity.

Despite professionals in every U.S. state and nearly 1,000 golf clubs by the early 1900s, the British continued to dominate the game. In 1913, a relatively unknown Massachusetts amateur named Francis Ouimet won the U.S. Open against the best of the British golfers. By turning back the great British players (including Ted Ray and Harry Vardon), Ouimet gave U.S. golf a huge boost, stoking more interest in the game than any other single event in its history.

Golf was changed dramatically again in the late 1950s with the advent of television coverage and the prominence of the undisputed king of the sport, Arnold Palmer. Palmer was perfect for the fledgling medium, and it was perfect for him. His telegenic triumphs finally brought golf to the masses and made it the fastest-growing sport in the U.S. for much of the 1960s.

Golf Tournaments

There are better than fifty tournaments each year on the U.S. professional golf tour; however, there are only four tournaments that rank as major championships: the Masters, the U.S. Open, the British Open, and the PGA.

The Masters
Held at the Augusta National Golf Club in Augusta, Georgia, this tournament is already rich in tradition despite the fact that it is the newest of the majors, having been first played in 1934. The most famous Masters tradition is the ceremonial green jacket that the defending champion slips on the current champion at the conclusion of each tournament. Much of the instant success of the tournament is due to Bobby Jones's involvement in its creation. Jones was a lifetime resident of nearby Atlanta and was one of the game's greatest talents.

The U.S. Open
Now regarded by some experts as the most important golf tournament in the world, the winner of the U.S. Open is assured golfing immortality. The United States Golf Association (the ruling body of golf in the U.S.) conducts the tournament and moves its location every year among the finest golf courses in America.

The British Open
The first major golf championship, dating back to 1861, the British Open was really the only golf championship up until the 1920s. The ruling body of golf in Great Britain, The Royal and Ancient, conducts the tournament each year as it rotates between six different courses.

The PGA Championship
As the tournament for the professional golfer in the U.S., the PGA Championship has never held the mystique that the other majors (founded on amateur golf) enjoy. It is traditionally the final major of the year.

Golf Situations

Golf, once the royal sport, has become the people's sport, and therefore, the sport of cliches. You'll be sure to see some of these situations if you choose to hit the links someday.

Situation: You hit the ball too far.
Phrase: "Hit a house!"
What it means: "I wish the ball would stop, really abruptly, really fast."
What not to say: "Hit that lady over there."

Situation: The ball you hit is headed toward someone's head.
Phrase: "FORE!"
What it means: "There is a flying projectile headed right for you."
What not to say: "Post card from Quayle!"

Situation: Your partner is putting first and has a similar putt as yours.
Phrase: "I'm gonna go to school on that one."
What it means: "I will study his putt and adjust mine accordingly."
What not to say: "Where'd you learn to putt like that?"

Situation: Someone in your foursome has hit a mediocre shot.
Phrase: "That'll play!"
What it means: "That's a terrible shot, but since I'm your partner I've got to support you."
What not to say: "Why don't you just go get us some beers?"

Golf Courses

To really impress, a Sports Literate golf fan should know the top courses in the game. You don't need to know much; just where they're located and maybe a little history.

St. Andrews. The home of golf, St. Andrews is the game's oldest continuously operated course. The "Old Course," as it is called, is one of the few remaining layouts that uses double greens (i.e., greens that are split into two parts with two flag sticks for two different holes).

Carnoustie. A regular site of the British Open Championship, Carnoustie is considered one of the toughest courses in the world. The winds here are typically very strong, making even the par-3 holes unreachable at times. Carnoustie is famous for its closing holes including the 17th and 18th that require the golfer to cross the Barry Burn twice on each hole.

Old Troon. Sometimes a British Open site, Troon is flatter and less difficult than Carnoustie. The most famous feature of this golf course is the par-3 8th hole, which plays about 150 yards to a heavily bunkered green that is so small it has been nicknamed the "Postage Stamp."

Pebble Beach Golf Links, Pebble Beach, Ca. This golf course is carefully pitched along the dramatic cliffs of the Northern California coastline. The Pacific Ocean is the main water hazard, coming into play on eight different holes. Many believe the 18th hole at Pebble Beach (characterized by the pounding Pacific Ocean to the golfer's left, as well as trees, bunkers, and a small green) to be the best finishing hole in golf.

Augusta National, Augusta, Ga. Located on the site of a former shrub nursery, Augusta National is famous for its azalea bushes, dogwood trees, and magnolias. The course hosts the Masters Tournament each year and was the creation of legendary golfer Bobby Jones.

Merion Golf Club, Ardmore, Pa. Instead of flagsticks on each green, Merion Golf Club uses brightly-colored wicker baskets, a tradition that instantly distinguishes this course from any other. Merion is also well-known for its deceptively easy holes including the mild-looking, 129 yard 13th hole whose bunkers have turned countless birdie plans into bogey.

Cypress Point, Carmel, Ca. With around 100 members, Cypress Point is one of the most exclusive golf clubs in America. Like neighboring Pebble Beach, Cypress Point looks rugged and deceptively simple. Cypress is famous for its dramatic beauty, including the par-3 16th where the golfer must clear an inlet of the Pacific Ocean to reach the green.

Muirfield Village Golf Links, Dublin, Oh. Much as Augusta National is the living tribute to Bobby Jones, Muirfield Village will be the lasting tribute to Jack Nicklaus. This is the site of the annual Memorial Tournament which is very near to attaining the status of a "major" golf tournament. The course and the tournament were both created by Nicklaus.

Cherry Hills Golf Club, Denver, Co. The mystique of Arnold Palmer began at the 1960 U.S. Open at Cherry Hills. Beginning the final day of play eight strokes off the lead, Palmer brought this golf course to its knees. He began play by reaching the par-4, 346 yard first hole with his drive. After a birdie at one, he proceeded to birdie the second hole, the third, the fourth, the sixth, and the seventh to score 30 on the front nine. His overall score of 65 for the day (the lowest final round score in the history of the U.S. Open) won the title and made Arnold Palmer a legend.

Names You Should Know

Walter Hagen: Known as "Sir Walter," the slick-haired Hagen won the PGA Championship a record five times (including four times in a row from 1924 to 1927). He was the first compelling personality to play the game and was famous for his impeccable dress.

Bobby Jones: Jones did what virtually no athlete has had the courage to try: he quit his game when he was at his peak. After winning more major championships than any other golfer at that time, Jones had his greatest year ever in 1930 at age twenty-eight. First he won the British Amateur, then the British Open, then the U.S. Open, and finally he completed the never-repeated "Grand Slam" of golf by winning the U.S. Amateur. The following day he retired from competitive golf forever.

Byron Nelson: Playing his best golf during World War II, Nelson won eighteen tournament in 1945 including a streak of eleven in a row. His earnings in 1945 doubled his take in 1944 when he won thirteen of the twenty-three events staged.

Ben Hogan: Hogan is one of the greatest competitors of professional sports. In 1949, while at the top of his game, Hogan was critically injured in a car accident. Many thought he would never play again, but the very next year he won a dramatic victory in the U.S. Open. He backed this up with five more major titles before his retirement.

Arnold Palmer: The man most credited with golf's tremendous popularity around the world is Arnold Palmer. His magnetic personality makes him the sentimental favorite in every event he plays and he will always be considered the "King of Golf." Even today, he consistently tops the list of endorsement money collected by athletes. The PGA Senior Tour has allowed a new generation of golf fans to see the legendary Palmer in action.

Lee Trevino: Raised in a one-room house on a cemetery in Dallas, Trevino overcame huge odds to become one of the greatest golfers of this era and the winningest golfer on the Senior Tour. Known for his antics on and off the course, "The Merry Mex" is also known as the man who prevented Nicklaus from winning the Grand Slam by holing out a chip shot on the 17th hole of the 1972 British Open.

Jack Nicklaus: The greatest golfer of all-time, Nicklaus has won more major championships than anyone else, and he is still the all-time leading money winner on the tour. While he continues to be a threat on the PGA tour, he has become the most feared competitor on the increasingly popular and lucrative Senior PGA Tour. Turning pro in 1959, no golfer has dominated the sport with such longevity.

Golf Glossary

Birdie: Scoring one under par on a hole.

Bogey: Scoring one over par on a hole. Two over par is called a *double bogey*; three over, a *triple bogey*, etc.

Bunker (a.k.a. *sand trap, beach, pot-bunker*): A strategically placed depression in the ground filled with sand. Usually found near greens or just off the fairway.

Dogleg: A golf hole that is not straight (i.e., it turns left or right before reaching the green).

Eagle: Scoring two under par on a hole. A hole-in-one on a par-3 is an eagle. (There is also a very rare *double eagle* for a three under par score on a hole.)

Hazard: An undesirable part of the course where a shot, although legal, would be very difficult. Ponds, creeks, and bunkers are all considered *hazards*.

Links: The course itself (specifically a seaside course, as in Scotland).

Making the Turn: A period of time in a round of golf between completition of play on the 9th green but before begining the 10th hole. (Traditionally the time for weekend golfers to grab a beer and/or a sandwich.)

Mulligan: An awful shot that is not added to a player's overall score upon the agreement of the other people in the foursome. Instead, the golfer tries again.

O.B.: Stands for *"Out of Bounds"* and refers to the course boundary. If a player's ball goes *O.B.*, he or she is assessed a one-stroke penalty and must replay the shot.

Par: A score that equals the standard established for the hole. Considered only a satisfactory accomplishment by a professional golfer.

Tee-Box: The area from which a golfer hits his or her first shot on each hole.

Shot Lingo
(From worst shot to best shot)

10. *Whiff:* Swing that completely misses the ball. The worst (and most embarrassing) shot in golf.

9. *Shank:* Bad mis-hit on the neck of the club that causes the ball to squib very little distance, but in an unpredictable direction.

8. *Scull:* Bad mis-hit that causes the ball to squib very little distance, but usually in a straight line.

7. *Worm-Burner:* Shot that goes straight but at a very low trajectory, skimming the top of the grass along the way.

6. *Sky:* Shot that goes straight but at a very high trajectory (a.k.a. *rainmaker*).

5. *Hook:* A well-hit ball that travels far but curves sharply to the left (very severe cases known as *duck hook*).

4. *Slice:* A well-hit ball that travels far but curves sharply to the right (very severe cases known as *banana ball*).

3. *Draw:* A well-hit ball that travels far but tails off left at the end.

2. *Fade:* A well-hit ball that travels far but tails off right at the end.

1. *Career-shot:* Perfect shot for the occasion.

Insider Quiz

1. When you hit a ball into the water, you should:
    - A. Take a two-stroke penalty and drop the ball near where it entered the water.
    - B. Take a one-stroke penalty, then hit the ball again from its original spot.
    - C. Wait until the other players aren't looking, then drop the ball wherever you want.

2. The best way to get a tee time in a major city is:
    - A. Call several courses ahead of time.
    - B. Make next week's tee time during this week's game.
    - C. Bribe somebody.

3. The most important clothing for a pro golfer is:
    - A. Sans-A-Belt pants.
    - B. A nice polo shirt.
    - C. A sponsor's logo.

4. The biggest pro money-maker in the last few years has been:
    - A. Greg Norman, due to strong second-place finishes.
    - B. Nick Faldo, due to the British Open and The Masters.
    - C. Arnold Palmer, due to Pennzoil and Hertz.

5. A golf tournament on television:
    - A. Lets you see legends go against each other.
    - B. Is a relaxing way to spend a Sunday.
    - C. Allows Cadillac to reach its target audience.

6. Spectators at golf matches:
    - A. May run ahead to the next green for good viewing.
    - B. May bring their own food and drink.
    - C. May not blow airhorns and throw toilet paper.

7. Pro golf's most harrowing hazard is:
    - A. The sand trap.
    - B. A lake, pond, or creek.
    - C. Payne Stewart's obnoxious, burnt-orange knickers.

7

Tennis

Tennis

 Of all major sports, tennis is one of the easiest to learn how to watch, but one of the hardest to learn how to play. The basic rule is that one person tries to get a ball past another person while keeping the ball in play. The scoring can be a little hard to pick up, and trying to learn how to play can be extremely frustrating, but tennis is basically an easy sport in which to become Sports Literate.

Tennis began as an indoor court game, like racketball or squash. The French called it "Jeu de Paume," or "game of the hand," and were its chief participants from the thirteenth century until the French Revolution, when the democratic wave destroyed all but one of the existing courts.

The sport made a debut in Shakespeare in the sixteenth century, in *Henry V*, with the French prince taunting young King Henry to war by accusing him of idling his time playing tennis. In fact, the British took to tennis tepidly until the introduction of lawn tennis, the modern form of the outdoor game. Lawn tennis was created in Wales in 1873 as an entertainment for a garden party, and quickly made its way to sophisticated summer parties in America.

Amateur tennis championships began throughout the U.S. and England in the 1880s. Amazingly, the pro tennis events as we know them today, with large prizes for the major tournaments and a sponsored tour between major events, did not exist until 1968. Prior to that time, the major events such as **Wimbledon**, the **U.S. Open**, and other major tournaments were open only to amateur players. Professionals went on barnstorming tours across various countries, generally making less than $100,000 per year. In the late '60s and early '70s, tennis became the sport of choice for the baby boom generation, and the result was larger purses, more TV coverage, and international media superstardom for greats such as Billie Jean King, Chris Evert, Jimmy Connors, and Bjorn Borg.

Tennis Fans

The Players' Box

Who's sitting in the box with the world's hottest tennis stars?

With the 30-year-old:

- Father
- Father's brother
- Ian Tiriac, tennis Svengali
- Coach, who is feuding with the father
- East European model girl-friend with illegitimate child
- Lawyer

With the 18 year old:

- Father
- Mother
- Brother
- Sister
- Electric guitar (a gift from Bon Jovi)
- Young coach

Call the Tennis Police

...when you see these violations on the court:

High-Toss Serve Guy
You know him. He throws the ball so high that weather balloons can track it. Meanwhile, you wait, and wait, and wait.

Just-A-Few-More-Practice Serves-Man
True, the first 99 practice serves were terrible, but he'll be ready after just one or two more.

Play-It-Over Woman
"Gosh, I couldn't tell, why don't we play it over?" Call the Tennis Police right away on this one, or you're in for a long, frustrating day.

Grunt Man
Yucch! He sounds like a caveman about to give birth. Tennis Police get extra arrest points if he grunts on every shot, including second serves. Jimmy Connors would have spent years in tennis jail for this offense.

The Talkers
"Well, it's such a nice day, why don't we take the Garden Club out to the tennis courts?" Funny how putting thirty feet and a net between some people can make them more interested in each other.

Paraphernalia Girl
She's got grip tape, she's got wristbands and a headband, she's got three rackets, she's got that little foam thing you stick at the base of your strings to stop them from vibrating—she's got six months in tennis jail.

Names You Should Know

Rene Lacoste: A Frenchman who was arguably the best player in the world in the '20s. His odd habit of gluing a small reptile onto his tennis shirt led to a craze in the preppy world which peaked in the early 1980s.

Bill Tilden: The best American player in the 1930s and the first pro player. He did much to popularize tennis with the masses.

Jack Kramer: Winner of Wimbledon in 1947, he did much to organize the United States pro tennis tour, an effort which culminated in pro players being admitted to the major amateur tournaments in 1968.

Rod Laver: "Rocket Rod," a small but powerful left-handed star from Australia, was the greatest player in the world in the 1960s. He led the Aussie charge of greats which included Ken Rosewall, Roy Emerson, and John Newcombe.

Jimmy Connors: Brought the U.S. back to the world forefront in the 1970s, after the Aussie invasion of the 1950s and '60s. Connors won two Wimbledons and five U.S. Opens, not to mention millions of dollars and a Playboy Playmate as a wife. When he was briefly engaged to Chris Evert in the mid-'70s, they were the most famous couple in the world.

Bjorn Borg: The cool Swede, winner of every major tournament but the U.S. Open, including five straight Wimbledons. Unmatched for consistency and burning desire to win.

John McEnroe: The feisty Long Island left-hander who seemed to rise to the top on sheer desire. Winner of three Wimbledons and four U.S. Opens.

Ivan Lendl: The Czech with the mechanical strokes and the amazing consistency, he has the Borg syndrome in reverse: he's won three U.S. Opens, but he's never won Wimbledon.

Helen Wills Moody: One of the most dominant players in the history of sport, winner of eight Wimbledon titles and seven U.S. Opens in the 1920s and '30s.

Billie Jean King: Six-time Wimbledon winner and participant in the event which perhaps marked the peak of tennis's fame: the 1976 contest against Bobby Riggs in the Houston Astrodome. Ms. King defeated Mr. Riggs, proving once and for all that women were as capable as men.

Althea Gibson: The first black woman to play at the U.S. Championships at Forest Hills, and, in 1957, the first black to win Wimbledon.

Chris Evert: She won Wimbledon three times and the U.S. Open six times, but Chris Evert will be remembered as much for her engaging personality and persistent temperament as her championships. The Arnold Palmer of women's tennis, she was attractive, poised, and lethal at the same time.

Martina Navratilova: Nine-time Wimbledon winner, perhaps the greatest female tennis star of all. One of the first women to add the bruising serve and net play of a man's game to the consistent strokes of a woman's, Martina became the embodiment of the "killer instinct" in the '80s. She has also won four U.S. Opens.

Great Feats

Borg's Five Wimbledons in a Row: When he began, he was a skinny young kid from Sweden. When he was finally knocked off by John McEnroe, he was in the same tax bracket as the Duchess of Kent, and a hell of a lot better known. Borg's streak capped the tennis boom, and McEnroe's victory signaled the beginning of the bust.

Martina's Nine Wimbledons: Not too many people brought up Helen Wills Moody's name in the the modern era, but in 1989 you would have thought she was still out there. Martina was going for the record of most Wimbledons, eclipsing Moody's eight. When she succeeded, Martina became, officially, the greatest women's tennis player of all time.

How to Watch Tennis

Tennis is above all a genteel sport. No yelling, lots of Rolexes, and strawberries and cream at Wimbledon. Even if you really like a player, you can't get away with waving one of those big "We're Number One" fingers.

Television always shows the "lady friends" or "special friends" of star tennis players. It's not quite like you and the husband in a nice little match of mixed doubles against the neighbors.

Tennis is one of the least likely sports that you'll attend in person, so you won't have to worry too much about viewing knowledge. Besides the sport isn't too tough to get the hang of. You just follow the little yellow ball until one player throws his racket up to the sky and falls to the ground saying, "Yes! Yes!" That one is the winner.

Glossary

Ace: A great serve that proves to be unreturnable.

Backspin: Flipping the wrist under as you hit the ball, causing the ball to bite backward when it hits the ground.

Deuce: A tie in the score of the game.

Drop Shot: A shot hit softly on the racket, so that it just barely clears the net, catching the opponent off guard.

Let: A serve that hits the net, but goes over.

Lob: A ball hit over an opponent's head while he is at net.

Serve: The method of starting play in which the first player throws the ball overhead and smashes it toward his opponent. Many of the great players have dominant serves.

Tantrum: What you throw when you disagree with a call.

Topspin: Flipping the wrist over as you hit the ball, causing overspin.

Volley: A return shot, often hit at net before the ball has been allowed to bounce.

Surfaces

You'll hear a lot of talk about the difference in playing the various surfaces of grass, clay, and hardcourt. In fact, the difference between surfaces is so great that, for example, a champion like Borg won five Wimbledons on grass, but never won the hardcourt U.S. Open. Here's a line up of the different surfaces and the major tournaments held on each:

Hardcourt (U.S. Open): A relatively fast surface. Works well for players who move quickly and have good net games.

Grass (Wimbledon): The fastest surface. Balls can skid and jump depending on the time of day and dryness of the ground. Players with big serves benefit.

Clay (French Open): The slowest surface. Favors the patient players with consistent ground strokes.

Insider Quiz

1. The best weapon in tennis is often:
    A. The smash.
    B. The lob.
    C. The tantrum.

2. Fans of Andre Agassi most admire his:
    A. Powerful topspin forehand.
    B. Consistent baseline game.
    C. Long, flowing hair.

3. A good way to prepare for a tough opponent is:
    A. Practice ground strokes until you can hit a solid backhand in your sleep.
    B. Use mental visualization to picture yourself defeating your opponent.
    C. Slash her tires.

4. The worst part of watching Wimbledon on TV is:
    A. Dealing with the early starting time.
    B. Watching the uneven bounces on the grass surface.
    C. Listening to Bud Collins pander to the Duke and Duchess of Kent.

5. The name Martina Navratilova is synonymous with:
    A. Powerful groundstrokes and quick volleys.
    B. A record number of Wimbledon titles.
    C. Goofy glasses and a big headband.

6. Bjorn Borg established the tennis tradition of:
    A. A two-handed backhand.
    B. Throwing the racket skyward after a win.
    C. Wearing sponsors' patches all over his shirt.

7. Tennis action is often stopped:
    A. At Wimbledon because there's a bird on the court.
    B. At the French Open because it's raining.
    C. At the U.S. Open because a guy named Richie from Queens is yelling "You suck!" at Ivan Lendl.

Boxing, Racing, Wrestling, & More

Boxing

There are those in the sporting world who say that boxing is the true best test of competition. All the accoutrements are stripped away. Just two men with a sliver of padding on each hand, pummeling away at each other until one man is left standing. No uniforms. No teammates. No coaches with headsets. Just competition, pure and simple.

For better or worse, boxing is one of the most popular of all sports, and the great heavyweight boxers have a bigger payday than any other athlete. Ties to the media on the one hand, and organized crime on the other, have led to the famous/infamous nature of the sport.

Increasingly, at the highest levels, the sport has been cleaned up, with major companies like Time/Warner acting as key players in promoting the best possible matches, often on pay-per-view television.

Each medium has had its superstar. From Joe Louis's "bum a month" radio knockouts to Muhammad Ali's television circuses, often involving Howard Cosell, the sport always seems to find the right man for the right time.

The brute agony and competition have caught the attention of artists, authors, and auteurs from Ernest Hemingway to Joyce Carol Oates to Martin Scorsese. In a high-tech age, there is something primordially compelling about boxing.

Names You Should Know

John L. Sullivan: The first nationally recognized boxer, around the turn of the century.

Jack Dempsey: Popularized boxing in the same way and at the same time that Babe Ruth popularized baseball. From the ring, to popular New York speakeasies, to the Hollywood movie screen, to Randolph Hearst's San Simeon parties, Dempsey was the most sought-after athlete of his day.

Gene Tunney: Beat Dempsey. Twice.

Joe Louis: "The Brown Bomber," from Detroit, who successfully defended the heavyweight title in twenty-five fights over twelve years, making him the most dominant fighter of all time.

Sugar Ray Robinson: A middleweight boxer (160-pound weight limit), in the 1950s, whose style and grace compared with Joe DiMaggio in baseball.

Muhammad Ali (Cassius Clay): The only heavyweight to gain the crown three times. The mix of Ali, television, and Howard Cosell made his career perhaps the most hyped in the history of athletics. He is still the most recognizable athlete in the world.

Sugar Ray Leonard: A charming Olympic champion who went on to fight some of the greatest fights of the late '70s and early '80s against Roberto Duran, Thomas Hearns, and Marvin Hagler.

Mike Tyson: A powerful young fighter whose relationships with Robin Givens, Don King, and Donald Trump added to his legend. Tyson seemed invincible until he was upset by little-known Buster Douglas.

George Foreman: Famous first for winning the title from Joe Frazier, then losing it to Muhammad Ali; famous second at age 42 for daring to take on svelte young champion Evander Holyfield.

Boxing Classics

From early black-and-white classics to the *Rocky* series to Martin Scorsese's modern black-and-white classic *Raging Bull*, Hollywood has loved the fights. Though the films tend to be filled with cliched characters and knockout punches that no human could survive in real life, these are some of the greatest sports movies made.

On the Waterfront (1954): Marlon Brando, Eva Marie Saint. Brando utters his famous "I coulda' been a contender" line in a classic study of a thug's life.

Somebody Up There Likes Me (1956): Paul Newman portrays real-life fighter Rocky Graziano, who rose from the slums of New York to become middleweight champion of the world.

Requiem For A Heavyweight (1962): A good film about corruption in the boxing world. Anthony Quinn stars as a washed-up fighter who receives career counseling from Julie Harris. Jackie Gleason, Mickey Rooney, and Muhammad Ali co-star.

Rocky (1976): Sylvester Stallone, Talia Shire. Academy Award-winning study in perseverance and motivation. Stallone wrote and starred in this film about an overachieving underdog who will not quit.

Rocky II-V (1979-1990): Sylvester Stallone, Talia Shire. Stallone takes the Rocky legend even further. A simple rule to remember: the higher the number, the less interesting the movie.

Raging Bull (1980): Robert DeNiro, Joe Pesci. Another Academy Award-winner, this one based on the life of middleweight Jake LaMotta, dealing with the struggles of a fighter with himself and his family outside of the ring. Often called the best film of the 1980s.

Racing

Races have always been an integral part of sports, going way back to the Greek and Roman games where athletes raced against each other for the amusement of the rulers, with a laurel wreath going to the winner. To provide some variety, races were devised involving horses, chariots, boats, and any other form of transportation.

As society became more sophisticated, so did racing. Horse racing grew into a billion dollar business and crude chariots evolved into high-powered automobiles capable of speeds in excess of 200 miles per hour. While the technology has changed, however, the basic aim of the sport has remained the same: go faster than the other guy.

Horse Racing

Called "The Sport of Kings" because of its appeal to royalty many years ago, horse racing today, with a few exceptions, could be labelled "The Sport of the Masses," since thousands of people flock to tracks all across the nation every week.

A few people here and there attend horse races for the sheer fun of it, reveling in the beauty of the animals and the thrill of competition. Most people, though, are in it for the bucks. Whether it's the big wheeler-dealer with a whole stable full of thoroughbreds or the average Joe who likes to "play the ponies," horse racing is a betting-person's sport.

Only bettors and breeders know the intricacies of horse racing, so give up any thoughts of becoming an instant pro. For you to get by, however, it's rather easy. If you go to the track, try to go with a friend who knows a little bit about the sport; simply plead ignorance and they will most likely be flattered to pass on what knowledge they have.

A few major horse races are televised. There are three major races that occur in the spring—the **Kentucky Derby** (the most prestigious), the **Preakness**, and the **Belmont**. It is very rare for one horse to win all three races; if this happens, it is referred to as **The Triple Crown**.

These races, and possibly the Breeder's Cup, are the only ones you need to worry about. The Sports Literate fan will do a little newspaper reading a week or so before the Kentucky Derby just to familiarize himself or herself with the names of the horses. The race itself is a piece of cake. Pick a horse you like, root for it, and see what happens. If your horse wins, you look like an expert. If your horse doesn't win, don't worry. A lot of other people guessed wrong too. And they probably lost a bundle.

Triple Crown Winning Horses

Sir Barton (1919), Gallant Fox (1930), Omaha (1935), War Admiral (1937), Whirlaway (1941), Count Fleet (1943), Assault (1946), Citation (1948), Secretariat (1973), Seattle Slew (1977), Affirmed (1978).

A Few Terms to Know

The Derby: The Kentucky Derby, horse racing's biggest event.

Homestretch: The last straightaway coming to the finish line.

Parimutuel Betting: Common at horse races, a system in which winners divide the net amount bet in proportion to their wagers.

Photo Finish: When the horses are so close that a photograph must be used to determine who won.

Post Time: Time for the race to begin.

Win / Place / Show: First/Second/Third place. A bettor makes money off these.

Auto Racing

Automobile racing is much easier to understand than horse racing, because there is no elaborate wagering system to deal with. Basically, a bunch of guys race around an oval track in amazingly fast and powerful cars, while the fans drink beer and hope for a spectacular crash (with no injuries, of course).

Auto racing is often referred to as the most popular sport in America, because of the number of races run and the number of people who pack the racetracks. There are a number of different types of auto racing, most of which are identified by initialed organizations (IMSA, CART, NASCAR, etc.) It's much easier to identify the type of racing by the type of car that is used. Take a look:

Type: Stock Car.
Description: Traditional, folk-hero type racing which is especially popular in the South.
Cars: Normal cars like Chevy Luminas are greatly modified, with huge engines and no back seats. Despite the technology, they do still resemble cars.
Famous tracks: Darlington, Atlanta, Talladega, Richmond, Daytona.
Famous drivers: Richard Petty, Junior Johnson, Geoff Bodine, Dale Earnhardt, Cale Yarborough, Bobby Allison.

Dale Earnhardt

Type: Indy Car.
Description: Named after the type of car driven in the Indianapolis 500, the most famous auto race in the world.
Cars: Very sleek and technologically advanced, they look like long tubes with wheels.
Famous tracks: Indianapolis. That's all you need to know.
Famous drivers: Mario Andretti, Bobby Unser, Al Unser, A. J. Foyt, Danny Sullivan, Rick Mears, Emerson Fittipaldi.

Type: Formula One.
Description: This is different because it takes place on a winding track or through the streets of a city.
Cars: Similar to Indy cars, though smaller and not as fast.
Famous tracks: Monaco, Le Mans, Long Beach, Ca.
Famous drivers: Jackie Stewart, Alain Proust, Nigel Mansell, Teo Fabi, Ayrton Senna.

Type: Drag Racing.
Description: One-on-one racing, down a straight track.
Cars: Either long, skinny "rail" dragsters, or "funny" cars, which look something like stock cars.
Famous tracks: Anywhere there's an audience and a strip of asphalt.
Famous drivers: Don "The Snake" Prudhomme, Shirley "Cha Cha" Muldowney.

A Few Terms to Know

Checkered Flag: Signifies the winner.

"Gentlemen, start your engines": Famous words said to racers before the start of the Indianapolis 500.

Green Flag: Signifies the start of a race.

Indianapolis 500: More than a race, this is an event. It's auto racing's Kentucky Derby, a Memorial Day race that assures the winner a place in racing history. Often referred to as *Indy*.

Pace Car: A car that drives in front of the race cars to start a race.

Pit Stop: When a car takes a break from the race for servicing and refueling.

Yellow Flag: Signifies a slowdown because of an accident.

Skiing

Skiing tends to be more of a participant rather than spectator sport, and most of the participants are pretty well-off, since it takes a good deal of money to afford a ski vacation or two a year.

Because of the clientele, status enters into skiing more than any major sport. If you're new to skiing, think of it as a posh mall on a mountain. You have to dress right, act right, and know the right terms.

Once marketed as a Club Med swinging kind of atmosphere, skiing is now being promoted as great family entertainment, as the baby boom market ages. The marketing challenge is daunting, and the explosive growth of ski resorts may belong to the James Bond era.

Names You Should Know

Most skiers are known only to readers of skiing magazines and TV viewers during an Olympic year. To appear well-versed, it wouldn't hurt to memorize the following names.

Jean-Claude Killy: A flamboyant Frenchman who won Olympic gold medals in 1968 in the downhill, the slalom, and the giant slalom. After turning pro, his name became synonymous with ski endorsements.

Franz Klammer: An Austrian who stunned the world with his frenetic, reckless downhill run to a gold medal in the 1976 Olympics.

Bill Koch: Won the first-ever U.S. medal in Nordic (cross-country) skiing.

Phil and Steve Mahre: Twin skiers from White Pass, Washington who helped elevate the level of U.S. skiing in the 1980s.

Jean Vuarnet: 1960 gold medalist more famous for the popular sunglasses he wore.

Ski Impostors

An integral element of skiing is to look the part on and off the slopes. Some people take this to the extreme by cashing in the skis and the afternoon of lessons in favor of a great outfit and a day in the lodge bar. Here's a guide to spot the most flagrant of these Ski Impostors:

Ski Impostor: Jake Norwood   **Age:** 23
Behavioral Pattern: Speaks too loudly (even for a bar), will always be seen with a drink in front of him to justify his annoying gestures.
Gimmick: Wears beach clothing (including shorts), to distinguish himself in a crowded bar.

Ski Impostor: Olaf Haugen   **Age:** 58
Behavioral Pattern: Always mixes outdated skiing terminology into conversations (e.g., "I made a huge sitz mark when I bit it off that hellatious jump").
Gimmick: The hokey Norwegian accent.

Ski Impostor: Misty Partmueller   **Age:** 31
Behavioral Pattern: Has perfect hair (even after wearing a stocking hat), never has a runny nose, and is continually applying lip balm.
Gimmick: A breakaway leg cast and crutches, and perfect fingernails.

Skiing Glossary

Binding: Device which holds the ski boot to the ski.

Bowl: A broad, cleared area of a ski slope characterized by steep sides and a steep beginning (i.e., shaped like a bowl).

Cross-Country Skiing: Like jogging on skis, this sport is more peaceful than downhill skiing, but just as tough. Also referred to as *Nordic Skiing*.

Downhill: A pattern of skiing or ski racing where the skier makes virtually no turns over a very long course.

Giant Slalom: A pattern of skiing or ski racing in which the skier makes a few turns over a reasonably long course.

Mogul: The mounds of snow on a ski run.

Schuss: Largely archaic verb that means to accelerate down the mountain as in: "Let's *schuss-boom* to the bottom of the hill."

Sitz: Archaic term referring to the depression in the snow that a skier would make after a fall. Prior to the age of snow grooming equipment, skiers were required to cover their own sitz marks.

Slalom: A pattern of skiing or ski racing where the skier makes many turns over a short course.

Snow Cat (or just *Cat*): The snow-grooming equipment used to smooth out runs following snowfall or heavy skiing.

Snowboarding

One of the fastest growing segments of the skiing market, snowboarders have become the skateboarders of the slopes. Most major ski resorts are now peppered with these snow surfers who zip in and out of the more leisurely and upscale customers. Snowboarders use a single board, which they control with body motion and deft feet. They often use the ski lifts, to the consternation of more traditional skiers.

Pro Wrestling

Though always popular among certain demographic groups, pro wrestling (often referred to as "rassling") has begun to enjoy immense popularity in the past few years. It bears little similarity to traditional wrestling, but through brilliant marketing and exposure on national television, pro wrestling has become quite profitable.

The #1 pro wrestling organization is the World Wrestling Federation (WWF). It has a number of televised shows, including *Saturday Night's Main Event*, and has made untold dollars from special pay-per-view events like *Wrestlemania*. The WWF is run by Vince McMahon (who also announces) and includes such superstars as Hulk Hogan, Randy "Macho King" Savage, and The Ultimate Warrior.

World Championship Wrestling (WCW) is owned by Turner Broadcasting. Although a cut below the WWF in fan support and popularity, the WCW is also quite profitable. Other organizations exist on the local level, with matches held in old armories, and the participants often a little out of shape.

Ten Rules to Learn About Pro Wrestling

1. It is not an Olympic sport.
2. BMW is not a sponsor.
3. The TV announcers are sometimes biased.
4. Wrestlers in face paint or masks are usually bad guys.
5. The refereeing is not very consistent.
6. Wrestling fans prefer beer to white wine.
7. Bad guys often beat good guys on national TV to set up a later rematch on a pay-per-view channel.
8. Certain women enjoy certain aspects of the sport and its scantily clad participants.
9. Only rule #10 matters.
10. Pro wrestling is fake.

Insider Quiz

1. Heavyweight boxer Mike Tyson is known for his:
    A. Fierce, never-say-die attitude.
    B. Vicious knockout punches.
    C. Arguments with Robin Givens.

2. The most memorable scene from the movie *Rocky* is:
    A. Rocky running up the stairs to the art museum.
    B. Rocky punching the slab of meat.
    C. Rocky stumbling around the ring yelling "Adrian!"

3. An out-of-work pro wrestler could probably find work as:
    A. A bouncer.
    B. A bodyguard.
    C. An actor.

4. Novice skiers enjoy watching pro skiers:
    A. Race down the hill at top speed.
    B. Cut in and out of moguls.
    C. Wipe out and face plant in the snow.

5. If you go to a stock car race, be sure to bring:
    A. A giant cushion.
    B. Binoculars.
    C. Enough beer to float a battleship.

6. A professional skier must always remember to:
    A. Get off to a good start.
    B. Finish strong.
    C. Hold his skis up, logo outward, on national TV.

7. In horse racing, a great horse is:
    A. Big and strong.
    B. Lithe and quick.
    C. One that wins you money.

Sports Geography

SPORTS GEOGRAPHY™

The Essential Guide To What Sports Are Hot In Your Area

- Bear Bryant: Still God in Alabama
- Knicks In The Game; Nets Are Lame
- Seattle's Mariners: Do They Exist?
- Baltimore After the Colts
- Hoops Crazy in Alaska
- Hot Rivalries in Idaho

Moving? Check Us First!

Printed in U.S.A. INDIA PATENTED 77214 ITALY 656879 JAPAN 41421B

Sports Geography

You like sports. You watch the local pro and college teams on TV and occasionally get to go to a game. You buy team souvenirs for yourself, your family, and your friends. You're into it. Then your boss gives you the news—you're being transferred to another city. You'll obviously continue to watch sports, but you don't know too much about the teams in your new area, and you don't want to look like a jerk. Sports Geography can help you make that transition. Check the capsules below on each of the fifty states plus the District of Columbia for things you need to know. It could be life-changing. Or at the least, keep you from making an embarrassing comment.

Alabama: Although there are no professional teams, football is incredibly popular. High school football coaches don't always teach, and the Alabama-Auburn game is the biggest event of the year. People still look skyward at the mention of late 'Bama coach/god Bear Bryant. The University of Alabama-Birmingham has a respectable basketball program. Among the state's legendary figures are baseball greats Willie Mays and Hank Aaron, and redneck NFL superstar Ken Stabler.
How to fit in: Let the outcome of the Alabama-Auburn game ruin your year.
Nice try: Ask someone who "The Bear" is.

Alaska: For obvious reasons, has no pro teams. The Iditarod dogsled race garners national publicity despite its limited appeal to those south of the 48th parallel. The Great Alaska Shootout is a preseason college basketball tournament that ESPN televises. Wealthy Anchorage residents have Seattle Seahawks season tickets and fly to games.
How to fit in: Rely on cable TV or a satellite dish for your info.
Nice try: Play golf.

The Iditarod

Arizona: The state has two solid Pac-10 schools in Arizona and Arizona State. The U of A basketball program is a national power and often sells out McHale Center. The Phoenix Cardinals of the NFL are the relocated St. Louis Cardinals, but despite the move they're still not very good. The Phoenix Suns are establishing themselves as one of the NBA's best, and are building a new arena. Baseball teams have made Arizona a favorite spot for spring training, which is quickly attracting vacationing fans, although a controversy over Martin Luther King, Jr. Day as a state holiday may put a damper on things.
How to fit in: Buy U of A season tickets.
Nice try: Actually care how the Cardinals do.

Arkansas: Remote state where the University of Arkansas in Fayetteville dominates nearly everything. With a move to the SEC, the school's hold on the state's football and basketball fans should grow even more. The University of Arkansas-Little Rock has built a respectable basketball program, but they still play little brother to the Hogs.
How to fit in: Wear a plastic Razorback on your head.
Nice try: Root for a school from Texas.

California: Almost needs its own book. Has virtually any sport you could imagine and at any level. Pro surfing? Got it. Skateboarding? Yep. Hockey? Of course. Has a number of the nation's best golf courses, including Spyglass Hill and Pebble Beach. Home of numerous tennis tournaments and prestigious horse races, especially at Santa Anita and Del Mar.

Southern California: Pro teams include baseball's legendary Los Angeles Dodgers and the San Diego Padres of the National League, and the American League's California Angels, who play in Anaheim. The Los Angeles Rams (also playing in Anaheim), the Los Angeles Raiders, and the San Diego Chargers are NFL teams, while basketball has the invariably tough Lakers and the invariably weak Clippers. The Kings play hockey and are the latest fan favorites with the addition of Wayne Gretzky, and the pro beach volleyball tour is quite popular. On the college level, USC and UCLA both have solid football programs, while UCLA and Loyola-Marymount grab most of the basketball press.

How to fit in: Get dressed up and go to a Lakers game.

Nice try: Get dressed up and go to a Clippers game.

Northern California: The Bay Area has solid pro franchises, but weaker college programs. The Oakland A's and San Francisco Giants are perennial baseball pennant contenders, and the San Francisco 49ers have won a number of Super Bowls. The Golden State (Oakland) Warriors are a decent pro basketball franchise, but the Sacramento Kings are candidates for sports euthanasia. San Jose has a new hockey team. Stanford and Cal-Berkeley both compete in the Pac-10, but rarely challenge for a title in any of the major sports. San Jose State and Fresno State have exceptional football programs, but are cursed geographically.

How to fit in: Hate any L.A. team.

Nice try: Think that the Stanford/Cal game really matters.

Colorado: The Denver Broncos are really the only game in town, though the University of Colorado football program has recently attained national prominence, and the Air Force Academy is always respectable. Basketball is a step behind, with the NBA Nuggets a constant disappointment, and CU's squad playing third fiddle to the ski team. Denver just got a pro baseball team, and the International golf tournament features a scoring system that only a CPA or a dyslexic could figure out.

How to fit in: Wear orange and blue to a Broncos game.

Nice try: Base your life around the Nuggets.

Connecticut: A real strong division of loyalty between New York and Boston, with an imaginary line probably drawn between Hartford and New Haven. Red Sox and Yankees fans toe this line more than anyone. The NFL Giants' success has won over most of the state, but basketball loyalties go to the Celtics, who still play games in the Hartford Civic Center. The Hartford Whalers have stolen some hockey fans from the Boston Bruins and New York Rangers. College sports are just OK, although

Yale football has the tradition and UConn basketball is nationally powerful.

How to fit in: Trek to Boston or New York for a sports weekend.

Nice try: Get really worked up over Yale games.

Delaware: Although you'd think this would be a state without much sports appeal, its location near Philadelphia makes it surprisingly hot. Fans regularly make the quick trip to Philly to support the Eagles, Sixers, Flyers, and Phillies. The University of Delaware has a good football team and helmets that look like Michigan's. Delaware Park Race Track is very popular.

How to fit in: Live and die with Philly sports teams.

Nice try: Root for a New York team.

District of Columbia: The Redskins have been a top-notch NFL franchise for years and always draw well and play well. The NHL Washington Capitals and the NBA Washington Bullets both play in the Capital Center in nearby Landover, Maryland, but neither has had much success lately. The most successful program in town has been Georgetown's nationally ranked basketball squad. Always among the country's best, the Hoyas also play in the Cap Center and enjoy good crowds. The constant call for the return of baseball to the nation's capital (the Senators have long since moved to Texas) is unlikely to produce results.

How to fit in: Expect the Capitals to choke.

Nice try: Expect the Bullets to win.

G-town's John Thompson

Florida: A booming sports state, with three of the top college football programs in America and a growing interest in the pros. The University of Miami and Florida State in Tallahassee are permanent Top Ten football teams, and the University of Florida in Gainesville is not far behind. College baseball is also superb, but basketball leaves something to be desired. Pro football's

Miami Dolphins get the nod over the Tampa Bay Buccaneers, but a hot rivalry has developed in the NBA between the Miami Heat and the Orlando Magic. Miami has a brand new baseball franchise, and Tampa has a new hockey team. Florida is also home to numerous bowl games (Gator Bowl, Orange Bowl), golf courses, and tennis courts, plus jai alai, greyhound racing, boating, fishing, and the Daytona 500.

How to fit in: Play a lot of sports, watch a lot of sports.

Nice try: Bet on the Tampa Bay Bucs to win the Super Bowl.

Georgia: Atlanta has three major sports teams, but none of them really get the job done. The football Falcons have been a disappointment for years, basketball's Hawks are known as the league's biggest underachievers, and baseball's Braves are perennial doormats, though they are showing signs of coming alive. Atlanta is still the big-time, however, and it has the 1996 Summer Olympics to prove it. In the college ranks, Georgia and Georgia Tech have solid football and basketball teams, and Georgia Southern in Statesboro is a Division I-AA football power. The Masters golf tournament held in Augusta is one of the hardest tickets in sports.

How to fit in: Go to pro games, but don't expect a win.

Nice try: Count on the Hawks to win in the playoffs.

Hawaii: Obviously, there is sailing, snorkeling, surfing, swimming, and anything else that comes with a tropical island. But there are also more conventional sports, and Hawaiians take their sports seriously. There is great interest in high school athletics, and even greater interest in the University of Hawaii. The Rainbow Warriors, who play in the Western Athletic Conference, have had good football and basketball teams, but it's hard for them to get national publicity when the games end too late for papers on the mainland. Hawaii is also the site of the Aloha Bowl, played on Christmas Day, and the NFL's all-star game, the Pro Bowl, played after the Super Bowl. Golf courses and tennis courts dot the islands.

How to fit in: Kick back and mellow out...until kickoff.

Nice try: Think that the weather and lifestyle don't affect the play of visiting teams.

Idaho: To most of America, Idaho sports may seem like the ultimate oxymoron or some part of David Letterman's monologue. Despite its sparse population, Idaho is a regional center for Big Sky conference events, and the rivalries are intense. Both Idaho and Boise State are among the nation's best in Division I-AA football, and they're also good in basketball. Though not usually as strong, Idaho State is competitive. The state also has great skiing in the Sun Valley area, and superb hunting and fishing.

How to fit in: Watch a Boise State game with its blue Astroturf.

Nice try: Say that squash is the ultimate test of manhood.

Illinois: Chicago is a great sports town. Along with New York, it's the last city to have two major league baseball teams (Anaheim doesn't count as L.A.). The Cubs play in venerable Wrigley Field with its ivy-lined outfield walls, while the White Sox have moved into a brand new Comiskey Park, which is a modern version of the old-time park. The NFL's Bears play in ancient Soldier Field, and the basketball Bulls and hockey Blackhawks play in even more ancient Chicago Stadium (which is an arena, not a stadium). Chicago-area college sports are just OK, with DePaul basketball continuing to be the best bet. Northwestern is always lame, so football-starved Chicagoans head across the Indiana border to watch Notre Dame, or cruise to Champaign-Urbana to see the University of Illinois. Downstate residents actually lean more toward St. Louis teams, and the Cubs-Cardinals rivalry is vicious.

How to fit in: Sit through a Bears game when it's ten below zero.

Nice try: Question Bears' coach Mike Ditka's toughness.

Satellite Bleacher Bums

Through the wonders of satellite television technology, the Chicago Cubs (via WGN), like the Atlanta Braves (via TBS), have created an audience of masochistic fans around the nation, willing to put up with the indignities of pulling for the nation's hard-luck baseball team. In return, fans get to wear a cute red and blue hat, moan about modern day lighting, and root for the same team that Bill Murray and Jim Belushi support.

Indiana: A great sports state. The Indianapolis 500 is Indiana's biggest event, but basketball is the state's true passion. The state high school tournament is a come-one, come-all event, with no size classifications. If you've seen the movie

Bobby Knight

Hoosiers, you get the idea. The college programs are solid, from Indiana University with the legendary Bobby Knight, to Purdue to Notre Dame to Ball State to Evansville to Indiana State, where Larry Bird played ball. While it may seem easy to dismiss football as less successful, don't forget about Notre Dame's awesome program in South Bend, as well as a fairly decent IU team. On the pro side of things, the teams are less successful. The NFL's Indianapolis Colts moved from Baltimore, and have never been as good as they were in Maryland, while the NBA's Pacers have been the epitome of an average franchise since they entered the league.
How to fit in: Call Bobby Knight's temper tantrums "character building."
Nice try: Malign basketball.

Iowa: College loyalties are somewhat split between Iowa and Iowa State, though Big Ten member Iowa has had the upper hand on Big Eight member Iowa State. Both schools have well-supported and well-run basketball, football, and wrestling programs. Iowa is a hotbed of wrestling, drawing good crowds for high school and college matches. Iowa girls' high school basketball still plays the traditional six-a-side, don't-cross-half-court style, and the state tournament is a hot ticket. This is an underrated sports state, often overlooked because of its lack of pro sports.
How to fit in: Be a basketball and wrestling fan.
Nice try: Say that your favorite wrestler is Hulk Hogan.

Kansas: Kansas City straddles the state line, but Missouri is the more dominant side, so we include most of KC's sports teams with Missouri. It is safe to say, however, that the Chiefs and Royals are the teams of choice for most Kansas residents. College hoops are very big, with Kansas (in Lawrence), Kansas State (in Manhattan) and Wichita State all fielding strong teams. Kansas, called KU, has a long tradition, starting with legendary coach Phog Allen and continuing through basketball's itinerant genius, Larry Brown. Fortunately, the basketball is good, because the college football is terrible. Both Kansas and K-State have weak programs, and often play each other for the right to claim seventh place in the Big Eight. Kansas is also the home of the headquarters of both the NCAA and the NAIA.

How to fit in: At a KU hoop game, wave your hands with the "waving wheat" and yell "Rock Chalk Jayhawk."

Nice try: Get all worked up over the Kansas-Kansas State football game.

Kentucky: Horse racing and horse breeding are Kentucky's claim to fame. In the heart of bluegrass country, nothing is more important. The Kentucky Derby is one of the greatest sporting events of all time, and Kentuckians take it very seriously. Basketball is a close second, though, and the University of Kentucky (UK) has a long, storied tradition going back to Adolph Rupp. The University of Louisville has actually had more success lately, but UK's huge arena, wealthy alumni, and history still make it top dog. Football is probably third in importance, but even when UK and Louisville are respectable, they must take a back seat to the hoop programs. Small schools like Eastern Kentucky, Western Kentucky, and Murray State have good athletic programs.

How to fit in: Enjoy mint juleps on Derby Day.

Nice try: Look puzzled when "My Old Kentucky Home" plays on Derby Day.

UK Basketball legend Coach Adolph Rupp

Louisiana: Bayou country is also sports country. Great hunting and fishing, as well as major athletic events. Louisiana State (LSU) basically owns the state, as boosters drive from all over to party (and watch) the football games. Recent tough years for the Tigers have frustrated loyal and maniacal followers. The LSU basketball program is superb and always attracts a crowd to its raucous arena, nicknamed the "Deafdome." Tulane, in New Orleans, just can't get its act together, but there are two superb black colleges, Southern and Grambling (whose coach, Eddie Robinson, is the winningest college coach of all time), as well as Southwestern Louisiana, and Northeast Louisiana who play good football. Pro sports are limited to the NFL's mediocre Saints, but as usual, New Orleans fans go insane at the games, partying and dressing up, so the actual outcome is often secondary. The Louisiana Superdome hosts the Sugar Bowl every New Year's Eve, and has been the site of numerous Super Bowls.

How to fit in: Dance in the aisles with the owner of the Saints.
Nice try: Go to an LSU game sober.

Maine:
Known primarily as an outdoor sports state, with some of the country's best canoeing, fishing, and hunting. Most professional sports loyalties lie with Boston teams. Hockey is popular, and, surprisingly, the University of Maine has an excellent baseball team, aided by a superb indoor practice facility.

How to fit in: Get dressing tips from L.L. Bean.
Nice try: Head to the beach for some volleyball.

Maryland:
Baltimore fans are still burning over the NFL Colts' midnight defection to Indianapolis, but still support baseball's Orioles (called "The Birds"). The Orioles have even captured the hearts of DC's long-suffering "bring back the Washington Senators" fans. The University of Maryland, near DC, has a decent football program and a basketball team that can't seem to regain the winning ways it had under former coach Lefty Driesell. Fans also travel to Landover to watch the NBA's Washington Bullets and the NHL's Capitals, and some people in the western part of the state root for Pittsburgh teams. Maryland is also big on horse breeding and racing (the Preakness) and is king of the small sports like lacrosse, fox hunting, and the state sport (believe it or not), jousting.

Colt Johnny Unitas

How to fit in: Watch the Birds and curse the Colts.
Nice try: Support Indianapolis.

Massachusetts: Very loyal following for the local pro sports teams. The Red Sox play in anachronistic but beautiful Fenway Park, and constantly surprise, but ultimately disappoint the fans. The legendary Celtics and hockey's Bruins share ancient, rundown Boston Garden, which probably won't be improved until visiting teams start winning a few games. The NFL's Patriots play down the road in Schaeffer Stadium, but locals are starting to figure out that all those traffic jams aren't worth it to see the team lose. Despite a proliferation of colleges, Boston College is the only school playing Division I-A football. College hockey is extremely popular, and Harvard, Boston U, Boston

College and Northeastern all have championship caliber programs. Springfield, in Western Massachusetts, is the home of the basketball Hall of Fame and the man who invented the game, Dr. James Naismith. Unfortunately, none of the state's colleges have been able really to reward the late Dr. Naismith with superb basketball.

Wade Boggs, Red Sox

How to fit in: Have yourself buried in Celtics or Red Sox colors.

Nice try: Support New York or L.A. teams.

Michigan: Detroit has four solid sports franchises, each playing in its own unique place. The NBA's Pistons regularly sell out the beautiful Palace at Auburn Hills north of the city, while the rebuilding Lions of the NFL play in the Pontiac Silverdome, one of the Teflon-roofed domes. Hockey's Red Wings play in the Joe Louis Arena, while baseball's Tigers still play in the same place they've always played in, Tiger Stadium, but the old park looks like it's headed for the wrecking ball. The University of Michigan in Ann Arbor and Michigan State in East Lansing compete in the Big Ten Conference and compete

well. Both have excellent football and basketball programs, and when they play each other, look out. Michigan Stadium in Ann Arbor is the largest on-campus stadium in America, and the

Wolverines average over 101,000 fans per game. The state also has a good hockey tradition, as well as superb outdoor activities during any season.

How to fit in: Scream for the Detroit Pistons, forgetting that they play more than thirty minutes away from downtown Detroit.

Nice try: Root for Ohio State.

Minnesota: A solid sports state. The Vikings and Twins play indoors in the Metrodome, which is called the "Homerdome" during baseball season. Both have had their shares of good times and bad, but are usually decent. The NBA expansion Timberwolves play in a new downtown arena, but often put patrons to sleep with their low-scoring games. The University of Minnesota usually has decent football and basketball teams. Hockey is also popular in the state, and while the NHL's North Stars are up and down, college hockey does very well and the annual high school tournament is a guaranteed sellout.

How to fit in: Make noise in the Metrodome so the other team can't hear.

Nice try: Insist that Vikings games were much more fun outdoors in the cold.

Mississippi: A small state with three Division I-A football programs. Mississippi (called "Ole Miss") in Oxford has had recent success, as has upstart Southern Mississippi in Hattiesburg. Mississippi State in Starkville has fallen on tough times, but will probably be back. The high school football is great, and has produced legends like Archie Manning, Marcus Dupree, and Walter Payton. Jackson State and Mississippi Valley College are good black college programs, the latter producing San Francisco 49er great Jerry Rice. Basketball and baseball are secondary in importance, though Mississippi State's baseball team is always a national contender.

How to fit in: Wave a Rebel flag at an Ole Miss game.

Nice try: Claim to dislike football.

Missouri: The pinnacle of Missouri sports came in the 1985 World Series when the St. Louis Cardinals played the Kansas

City Royals. Affectionately dubbed the "Interstate 70 Series," the event polarized the state. Both cities are great baseball towns. Unfortunately, the football Cardinals left for Phoenix, leaving the Kansas City Chiefs as the only NFL franchise in the state. Hockey's St. Louis Blues help make the baseball off-season tolerable. Big Eight member Missouri (called Mizzou) has a good basketball team, but a football team that's a constant disappointment. Thanks to support from Anheuser-Busch, the St. Louis area is the nation's hottest soccer spot.

How to fit in: Drink Bud and hate the Cubs.

Nice try: Think Mizzou has a shot at the Big Eight football title.

Montana: Obviously, there is no big-time professional sports presence, but much like Idaho, the local colleges have a good following. Also like Idaho, they compete in the Big Sky Conference, which, although lacking in exposure, is always entertaining. Montana (in Missoula) and Montana State (in Bozeman) are usually near the top of the league in football and basketball, and sparks fly when the two meet. Outdoor recreation is extremely popular, both in summer (boating, fishing) and winter (skiing, hunting).

How to fit in: Drink a few longnecks before and after the UM-MSU game.

Nice try: Wear a sportcoat and tie to the UM-MSU game.

Nebraska: You can sum it up in three words: Go Big Red. The University of Nebraska football program has an amazing hold on the state's fans, uniting bankers and farmers, cowboys and city slickers. Certain road signs direct you not to "Lincoln" but to "NU Football Stadium." If you can't make it to a game, you must have a TV or a radio on. The big games are against Big Eight rivals Oklahoma and Colorado. Basketball is a minor sport in Nebraska. Omaha hosts baseball's College World Series at Rosenblatt Stadium. A few fans in the western part of the state support Colorado teams, but NU football is where it's at.

How to fit in: Wear red.

Nice try: Run errands on game day.

Nevada: Despite the fact that the state has no professional sports teams (though some would mention Nevada-Las Vegas basketball), Nevada could be the sports capital of the nation. Why? Gambling, of course. Las Vegas is the center of oddsmaking in the United States, and the only place where you can legally bet on any sport. It is also the site of many big-time boxing matches. On the field and the court, the aforementioned UNLV has arguably the best basketball team in the nation year in and year out, but is also under constant NCAA scrutiny for various violations. The smaller University of Nevada Reno has a solid Division I-AA football program in the Big Sky Conference.
How to fit in: Make the "shark sign" for UNLV coach Jerry "Tark the Shark" Tarkanian.
Nice try: Lead an anti-sports-gambling crusade.

New Hampshire: Like Maine and Rhode Island, New Hampshire has a strong Boston orientation. You'll find a number of Bruins, Celtics, Patriots, and Red Sox fans, particularly in the southern part of the state. The University of New Hampshire is small-time in most sports, but plays competitive ice hockey. There are also a number of popular ski areas.
How to fit in: Yell and scream for Boston teams.
Nice try: Get all fired up for a New Hampshire-Vermont game.

New Jersey: Bordering on New York and Pennsylvania makes this an important sports state. Folks in the northern part of the state root for New York City teams, while those south of Trenton root for Philly clubs. The Meadowlands in East Rutherford—across the Hudson River from NYC—is a multisport complex with horse and auto racing, plus Giants Stadium (home of the NFL's New York Giants and New York Jets) and Brendan Byrne Arena (home of hockey's New Jersey Devils and everybody's favorite doormat, the NBA New Jersey Nets). Rutgers is the only Division I-A college football team in the state, and they're just OK. Seton Hall has built a solid basketball program and competes in the Big East. Atlantic City has become a sort of Vegas of the East Coast, with big-time boxing matches.
How to fit in: Start barroom arguments about New York vs. Philly.
Nice try: Buy season tickets to the Nets.

New Mexico: Unlike neighboring Arizona, there are no professional sports franchises in the state. Both the University of New Mexico in Albuquerque and New Mexico State in Las Cruces have good basketball teams and poor football teams. UNM hoop games are often sold out at its arena, affectionately dubbed "The Pit." The state also has a number of superb ski areas.

How to fit in: Make "Lobo" signs with your fingers at New Mexico games.

Nice try: Bet heavily in favor of the New Mexico State football team.

 New York: You name it, you got it. From skiing and hunting upstate, to boxing and basketball in Manhattan's legendary Madison Square Garden, New York is a state that loves its sports. The professional teams are at opposite ends of the state, New York City and Buffalo. The teams in the Big Apple are always in the media spotlight and tend to get more publicity than they often deserve. The NFL Giants and baseball's Mets have had the best teams lately, while the NFL Jets and baseball's once-mighty Yankees have endured rough seasons. In the NBA, the Knicks do OK, but can't seem to get over the hump (translation: finish ahead of the Celtics or 76ers). NYC also has two hockey teams—the Rangers (who play in the Garden) and the Islanders (who play on Long Island)—that are usually competitive. Buffalo has the NFL Bills and hockey's Sabres, plus a minor league baseball franchise that sets attendance records. New York's college football is not very impressive; only Syracuse contends seriously. Cornell plays in the Ivy League and Army is just average. A number of smaller schools compete very well. Basketball is another story. New York City has a great hoops tradition, and it's seen in the excellent high school play as well as college programs like St. John's. Again, the nod for best college team goes to the school upstate, Syracuse, which is often among the Top Five in the country and packs in the fans.

How to fit in: Bet for the Mets and against the Knicks.

Nice try: Support former Yankee dictator George Steinbrenner.

North Carolina: A diverse state, with lots of sports to keep it hopping. Basketball is still king of the colleges, with four major programs at Duke, North Carolina (called "Carolina"), NC State (called "State"), and Wake Forest. Carolina's program has the tradition, but Duke has been more successful lately. All four schools have rabid rooters, but Duke's fans are known nationwide for their creative (and sometimes insensitive) taunting of opponents. Football programs vary from year to year, with Carolina or State usually on top. A pro football franchise is rumored, but pro fans will have to content themselves with Charlotte's Hornets, an NBA expansion franchise that draws well, and the minor league baseball Durham Bulls, seen in the movie *Bull Durham*. The state also has great golf and fishing, and the stock car racing might be the best in the country. The Petty family, legendary Lee, his even more legendary son Richard, and Richard's son Kyle, are from Randleman, and there are condos for sale on the first turn of the Charlotte Motor Speedway.

How to fit in: Take your basketball seriously. Very seriously.
Nice try: Wear light blue (known as "Carolina Blue") at Duke.

North Dakota: Not a lot going on, but North Dakota State has topnotch football and the University of North Dakota has excellent hockey. NDSU is a perennial Division II football powerhouse with great fan support. Those close to the Minnesota border often make the trek to the Twin Cities to watch pro teams there.
How to fit in: Follow the NDSU Bison around the country at playoff time.
Nice try: Lobby for a major league baseball franchise.

Ohio: Professional loyalties are split between Cleveland and Cincinnati. The baseball teams (the Indians and the Reds) are in different leagues, so there isn't a real rivalry, and the Indians are not usually competitive, while the Reds are tough. The football teams (the Browns and the Bengals), on the other hand, are not only in the same division, but they have the same colors, so games can be real intense and real ugly. The Cleveland Cavaliers are the only NBA franchise in the state. Ohio State

University is the unifying force. The Buckeyes draw over 80,000 fans per game to Columbus for football, and they do well in hoops too. They are a big-time university in a powerful conference (the Big Ten). Miami University (called Miami of Ohio) is responsible for turning out some of the greatest football coaches of all time. The Pro Football Hall of Fame is located in Canton.

How to fit in: Cheer the OSU band as they do the "Script Ohio" formation.

Nice try: Root for Michigan.

Oklahoma: A classic case of big-city versus rural. Oklahoma University (OU) is located in Norman, near Oklahoma City, and is just too dominant for its country counterpart, Oklahoma State (OSU) in Stillwater. OSU does a solid job in both basketball and football, but OU is usually in the Top Ten nationally. Oklahoma State is nationally ranked in baseball and wrestling, but when the money matters, bank on OU. Tulsa is clearly the odd man out

Oklahoma Wrestling

in this state, despite decent athletic teams. Pro fans probably support Texas clubs, but the "T" word is unmentionable during the college seasons. Oklahoma is also home to the Cowboy Hall of Fame, and rodeo is a big-time attraction.

How to fit in: Have a car horn that plays "Boomer Sooner," the OU fight song.

Nice try: Claim to be a friend of ex-OU linebacker/goofball Brian Bosworth.

Oregon: Oregon sports can be summed up in one word (or is it two?)—Trail Blazers. The Blazers, as they're called by Oregonians, own the state, and especially Portland. Home games have been sold out for years, and fans pay thirteen dollars to watch on big screens in locations around the state. On the collegiate scene, University of Oregon football has achieved respectability and is miles ahead of a pathetic Oregon State program. Nike is headquartered in Beaverton, and there is substantial interest in running, particularly in Eugene, where many world-class athletes train. The Columbia River Gorge is known for having some of the best windsurfing in America.

How to fit in: Say: "How about those Blazers?"

Nice try: Criticize a local sports figure.

Pennsylvania: A great sports state, which
is really split between East and West and cen-
tered around Philadelphia and Pittsburgh. The
one exception to this is Penn State, located in the
middle of the state and pulling football fans from
all over. The Nittany Lions have had a solid program from Rip
Engel's days through the current era of legendary Joe Paterno,
and they're always a national power. The University of Pittsburgh tries hard, but can't quite maintain consistency, while
Temple flounders and Penn plays in the Ivy League. In basketball, it's the city game, with Villanova, Temple, and LaSalle
dominating in Philly, and Pitt, a Big East member, holding court
in the West. In the pro ranks, the Philly-Pittsburgh rivalry holds
true. You're for the Steelers or the Eagles, the Pirates or the
Phillies, the Penguins or the Flyers, and games are a matter of
life and death. Only the NBA's Philadelphia 76ers lack an in-
state rival. Pennsylvania's sports history is full of glorious
names—Wilt Chamberlain, Arnold Palmer, Joe Namath, Tom
Gola, Joe Montana—and has had much to do with the early
development of college and professional sports.
How to fit in: If a player is dogging it, boo him!
Nice try: Support New York teams.

Rhode Island: Its proximity to Massachusetts makes the
pro sports orientation pro-Boston. Brown University is average
even for the Ivy League, but Providence College competes in
basketball's Big East Conference, and occasionally will contend
for an NCAA title. The Tennis Hall of Fame is located in
Newport, and that seaside city is also the site of numerous
regattas. Things really jump if Newport is fortunate enough to
host an America's Cup race.
How to fit in: Go to a regatta and enjoy the atmosphere.
Nice try: Go to a regatta, scream, and wave a big foam "We're
Number One" finger.

South Carolina: Despite the possibility of an NFL expansion franchise, the real focus in this state is on college football.
The state is pretty much split between Clemson and the University of South Carolina (called "USC" here and only here). Clemson
is usually a Top Ten team and has had the edge on USC recently.

The Citadel in Charleston has an historic tradition, but lags behind the other two schools. Furman is a good Division I-AA school. Clemson basketball is also very tough, and the school is known for its rabid fans who wear as much orange clothing as is physically possible. There is golf and tennis at Hilton Head, and lots of auto racing, the most famous track being Darlington.
How to fit in: Treat a Clemson-South Carolina game as a matter of life or death.
Nice try: Taunt a Clemson fan about his orange outfit.

South Dakota: Kinda' dry without a satellite dish to keep you aware. Its small population base, makes it tough to sustain a pro or college sports program. High school sports are followed closely, as are South Dakota and South Dakota State, but the intensity of the North Dakota schools just isn't there. The hunting and fishing are excellent.
How to fit in: Stay indoors in the winter and watch ESPN.
Nice try: Become a surfer.

Tennessee: The state is really three regions, dominated by three major cities: Knoxville in the east, Nashville in the center, and Memphis in the west. The one common denominator is UT (University of Tennessee) football. The Knoxville school's Neyland Stadium packs in over 90,000 fans for Southeastern Conference action. Memphis State clearly plays second fiddle, but their hoop program is better, and the city hosts the Liberty Bowl every year. Vanderbilt, in Nashville, is an academic school stuck in the heart of football mania, and their record shows it. Vandy basketball, though, is always respectable. There are a number of smaller schools with excellent athletic programs: Austin Peay, East Tennessee State, Middle Tennessee State, and Tennessee-Chattanooga.
How to fit in: Wear orange and sing along to "Rocky Top" at UT games.
Nice try: Bet your savings on Vanderbilt football having a winning record.

Texas: Another great sports state, with plenty of options for fans. Dallas, Houston, and San Antonio all have pro teams, and a number of colleges compete in the Southwest Conference.

Dallas has the legendary Cowboys who are starting to rebuild after a few down years, plus basketball's Mavericks and the Texas Rangers, who play baseball in nearby Arlington. Houston's Oilers (who play in the Astrodome) have been a pretty good team, as have the NBA Rockets. San Antonio has the basketball Spurs, who are quickly turning into one of the NBA's elite teams. College basketball is fairly weak (other than Texas, Houston and Texas-El Paso), but the football is good, when teams aren't on NCAA probation. Texas (Austin), Texas A&M (College Station), Baylor (Waco), and the Univerity of Houston are usually tough. Rice (Houston), SMU (Dallas), TCU (Fort Worth), and Texas Tech (Lubbock) usually vary from average to lame. A number of smaller schools (like Texas A&I) play good ball, and the high school programs in the state (like Odessa Permian) are as good as some states' college programs. Texas' size allows a number of different outdoor sports, from hunting to surfing.

How to fit in: Make a "Hook 'em Horns" sign at UT or stand for the entire game at Texas A&M.

Nice try: Root for Oklahoma.

Utah: A surprisingly decent sports state, despite its relative isolation. The only professional team is the NBA's Utah Jazz, who are building a new arena. Brigham Young University is a national power in football and draws huge crowds. There are four solid major college basketball programs, with BYU, Utah, Utah State, and Weber State (pronounced WEE-ber). The state is also known for having the best powder skiing in the country.

How to fit in: Talk about the big game at the "Y" (BYU).

Nice try: Dress sloppily and get really drunk at a BYU game.

Vermont: One of the few states where the state university does not field a football team. The University of Vermont, however, does have a basketball team, a good hockey team, a great ski team, and a cool nickname (the Catamounts). They could also field a superb hackysack or frisbee squad. The state has great mountain areas for skiing and mountain-climbing.

How to fit in: Be apathetic about U of V sports.

Nice try: Look for a great game of hoops at Bennington College.

Virginia: The state has no major pro franchises, but there is a strong pull from DC for the Redskins. The University of Virginia (UVa) has topnotch football and basketball, as well as a gorgeous campus designed by Thomas Jefferson. There are a number of smaller schools that have good athletics: Virginia Tech, James Madison, William and Mary, Richmond, VMI, Liberty, Virginia Commonwealth, and Old Dominion. The state also boasts numerous golf courses, auto racing tracks and minor league baseball teams.

How to fit in: Go to a UVa football game dressed in a blazer and a tie.

Nice try: Go to a UVa football game dressed like Thomas Jefferson.

Washington: Seattle is a big-time sports town, and perhaps the best in America at supporting a major college football program and a pro football team. On a weekend in October, it's not unusual to find more than 70,000 fans packing picturesque Husky Stadium on Saturday, and then see 65,000 inside the Kingdome on Sunday to root on the Seahawks. The NBA's Sonics are usually respectable, but baseball's Mariners are permanent pictures of futility. People on the east side of the state are more likely to support Washington State University, but the Cougs have played weak sister to the Huskies for years. The Seafair Hydroplane races during the summer are a huge event.

How to fit in: Call the Huskies the "Dawgs."

Nice try: Believe that the Mariners have a shot at a pennant.

West Virginia: The University of West Virginia in Morgantown has the run of the state, and their football and basketball programs have been respectable enough to garner a great following. Pro fans split their loyalties between Pittsburgh, Washington DC, and Baltimore. Charles Town and Shenandoah Downs are popular horse racing tracks, and the White Sulphur Springs/Greenbrier resort is a famous destination where FDR used to hang out and Sam Snead was the golf pro.

How to fit in: Go insane at WVU football games.

Nice try: Insist that polo is the only real sport.

Wisconsin: Another good sports state in the upper Midwest. Loyal fans support the NBA Milwaukee Bucks despite the worst uniforms this side of the Soviet Union. Baseball games are a treat, because the Brewers are good and the concession stand food is the best in the business. The legendary Green Bay Packers represent the smallest city in the NFL, but they do play a number of games in Milwaukee as well. The University of Wisconsin at Madison has been at the bottom of the Big Ten for years, but continues to draw fans. The small Wisconsin schools like LaCrosse and Stevens Point play solid football and basketball. Hockey is also a big sport.

How to fit in: Wear cheeseheads and eat brats.
Nice try: Book a Rose Bowl trip for UW.

Wyoming: The University of Wyoming (in Laramie) is about it for this sparsely populated state. The success of the Denver Broncos has cut into the U of W's attendance, but the locals still support Cowboy football and basketball. Most of the state's reputation comes from outdoor recreation: hunting, fishing, skiing, and camping.

How to fit in: Party with friends before a Wyoming football game.
Nice try: Wear a blazer, tie, and loafers to a Wyoming football game.

War Memorial Stadium, Laramie, Wyoming

10

The List

Improving Your IQ

There is no way to gain a high Sports IQ overnight. It takes years of sitting in front of the TV, soaking up sports knowledge along with the beer, to become an expert. But, as we said before, you don't have to become an expert; you need only to become Sports Literate, and accomplishing that is not as difficult as you may think.

The easiest way to increasing your IQ is to read. The sports pages of your local paper are a good place to start. They'll contain most of the national news you'll want, like who's in first place in the American League West or how many points Clyde Drexler scored the night before. Often, however, local papers won't have the score of a game you want to know about. Or for some reason, they'll get a score wrong. That's why you need to take a look at some other publications to help you along.

USA Today: Has a great, easy-to-read sports section. It may be "McPaper" for news, but it's "McWinner" for sports.

The Sporting News: Trying to upgrade its image from just a baseball magazine, and doing a good job. Well-written columns, good info.

Sports Illustrated: The Lexus of sports magazines. Great photos, great personality profiles, great writing. Don't read this for facts, read it for analysis and feature stories.

Sport and *Inside Sport*: Decent companion volumes to other sports publications.

The National: Big fantasy, small reality. A daily national sports paper that tried to establish itself in January, 1990. Despite good writing, it went out of business in June of 1991.

New York Times: Good analysis, but hurting in the facts department. Also, it misses a lot of the later West Coast scores.

Television, of course, is the most obvious medium for improving your Sports IQ. Many commentators, however, assume you know a certain amount about sports, so they are not necessarily the best sources for beginners.

ESPN: The all-sports network. You have to wade through the month-old logging competitions and the fitness shows, but if you want sports, this is the channel to turn to. The *SportsCenter* show has all the highlights you'd ever want, and Roy Firestone's *SportsLook* has the best sports interviews in the world.

CNN: Ted Turner's all-news channel also does a great job with sports. While not quite as thorough as *SportsCenter*, CNN's nightly sports shows are the next best thing on TV. Also check Turner's *Headline News* channel at 10 till and 20 after for sports updates.

The Networks: ABC, NBC, and CBS have most of the big games and the big names. They've also got more hype than a Papal visit to Latin America. Your best bet is to skip the analysis and the hour-long pre-game hype and just watch the event. Many people watch network events while listening to the radio description. For a break from the typical sports announcer, try listening to the irreverent Bob Costas or the witty Dan Dierdorf, both outstanding performers in a profession full of mediocrity.

Once you've become comfortable reading and watching sports, it's time to start talking. That's where The List comes in. With over 300 terms and names, it's the perfect way to pump up your Sports IQ, or to get started on the road to Sports Literacy.

Boston's Roger Clemens:
You better know who he is.

The List

We left off the obvious terms, like "quarterback" and "home run." These are terms most Americans have grown up with, terms the country has gone to war to protect. We have, however, included "quarterback sneak" and "inside-the-park home run," fairly common terms that not everyone understands. We've also left off dozens, if not hundreds, of great ballplayers. We've listed the ones you need to know to be Sports Literate. You must know Joe Montana; you must know Babe Ruth. You must know Magic Johnson, Wayne Gretzky, and Nolan Ryan. They're the high visibility players that everyone will assume you know. Anyone else is gravy.

Take a look at The List. Go over the terms and names and see how many you recognize. Then see how many you can explain. Add up your total and see how you compare with the chart on page 160. We don't guarantee anything other than the fact that if you know the meaning or significance of every name on this list, you will be Sports Literate, on your way to a high Sports IQ.

Pro Football Names

Bo Jackson , football star who also plays baseball.

AFL
Baltimore Colts
The Boz
CFL
Cunningham, Randall
Davis, Al
Ditka, Mike
Elway, John
Esiason, Boomer
Jackson, Bo
Landry, Tom
Lombardi, Vince
Montana, Joe
Monday Night Football
Namath, Joe
NFL
Oakland Raiders
Payton, Walter
Perry, Refrigerator
Pro Bowl
Rice, Jerry
St. Louis Cardinals
Shula, Don
Simpson, O.J.
Super Bowl
USFL
Walsh, Bill
WFL
WLAF

College Football Names

Bowl Games
Bryant, Bear
Death Penalty
The Gipper
Hayes, Woody
Heisman Trophy
Holtz, Lou
Ismail, Rocket
NAIA
NCAA
Orange Bowl
Paterno, Joe
Polls
Probation
Prop 48
Redshirt
Rockne, Knute
Rose Bowl

Penn State's Joe Paterno, major college football's winningest active coach

Football Terms

Blitz
Bomb
Bootleg
Call for a Measurement
Clipping
Draw Play
Fair Catch
Goal Line Stand
Hail Mary
Holding
Interference
In the Grasp
Late Hit
Lateral
Line of Scrimmage
Luxury Box
Onside Kick
PAT
Play Action

Quarterback Sneak
Quick Kick
Rollout
Roughing The Passer
Sack
Safety
Shotgun
Sudden Death
Two-Minute Drill
Two-Minute Warning
Two-Point Conversion

Notre Dame coaching legend Knute Rockne

Pro Basketball

ABA
Abdul-Jabbar, Kareem
Barkley, Charles
Bird, Larry
Bol, Manute
CBA
Chamberlain, Wilt
Erving, Julius "Dr. J"
Ewing, Patrick
Johnson, Magic
Jordan, Michael
Laimbeer, Bill
Lee, Spike
Olajuwon, Hakeem
Riley, Pat
Robinson, David
Russell, Bill
Thomas, Isiah
Worthy, James

The incredible Michael Jordan

College Basketball

Alcindor, Lew
Final Four
Knight, Bobby
Krzyzewski, Mike
Maravich, Pete
NIT
Smith, Dean
Tark "The Shark"
Thompson, John
Walton, Bill
Wooden, John

Bill Walton rejects a shot

Basketball Terms

Baseline
Double Dribble
Final Four
Goaltending
Illegal Defense
In the Bonus
Jump Ball
The Key
Man-to-man
Offensive Foul
One and one
Press
Slam Dunk
Technical Foul
Three Point Shot
Three Second Violation
Traveling
24 Second Clock
Zone

Magic Johnson takes it to the hoop

Handy Guide to Watching the NBA

Player You Cannot Hate: Michael Jordan
Player You Must Hate: Bill Laimbeer
Most Likely to Get the Call: Magic Johnson
Hotdog: Dennis Rodman
Baby-Faced Killer: Isiah Thomas
Star of the Future: Scottie Pippen

Team of the Past: Boston Celtics
Teams of the Present: Chicago Bulls, L.A. Lakers
Teams of the Future: Phoenix Suns, Portland Trail Blazers
Team That Always Chokes: Atlanta Hawks
Teams That Suck: Denver Nuggets, Sacramento Kings

Baseball Names

Aaron, Hank
Canseco, Jose
Clemens, Roger
Cobb, Ty
DiMaggio, Joe
Doubleday, Abner
Gehrig, Lou
Mantle, Mickey
Martin, Billy
Mays, Willie
Oh, Sadaharu
Rose, Pete
Ruth, Babe
Ryan, Nolan
Steinbrenner, George
Williams, Ted
Young, Cy

Yankee great Babe Ruth

Baseball Terms

Balk
Bullpen
Bunt
Change Up
Curveball
College World Series
Designated Hitter
Double Play
Dugout
ERA
Error
Golden Glove
Green Monster
Ground Rule Double
Knuckleball
LCS
Minor Leagues
No-Hitter

On Deck
Perfect Game
Pinch Hit
Pine Tar
RBI
Reliever
Sacrifice
Save
Screwball
Slider
Spitball
Squeeze
Steal
Triple Play
Walk
Warning Track
World Series

Hockey

Assist
Blue Line
Check
Faceoff
Gretzky, Wayne
Hat Trick
Howe, Gordie
Hull, Bobby
Icing
Lemieux, Mario
"Miracle on Ice"
Orr, Bobby
Penalty Box
Penalty Shot
Power Play
Puck
Pull the Goalie
Slapshot
Stanley Cup

Words You Won't Hear at a Hockey Game

Montessori
Thank you
Haberdashery
Brown vs. The Board of Education
What's so great about Quebec?
Peggy Fleming
Police brutality
Tanqueray
Gretzky sucks
Ultra-brite smile

Soccer

Corner Kick
Free Kick
Goalie
Header
Hooligans
Indoor Soccer
Injury Time
Maradona
Pele
Penalty Kick
Red Card
Throw In
World Cup
Yellow Card

Bad Things About Soccer

1. Players often referred to as "the lads."

2. No time outs cuts down on fans' beer runs.

3. Settling tie games by penalty kicks is like settling an overtime basketball game with free throws.

Golf

Augusta, Ga.
Birdie
Bogey
British Open
Bunker
Caddie
Chip
Divot
Eagle
Fairway
Green Jacket
Hook
Links
Nicklaus, Jack
Palmer, Arnold
Par
Pebble Beach
PGA
Slice
St. Andrews
Stewart, Payne
The Cut
The Masters
U.S. Open

Tennis

Ace
Agassi, Andre
Backhand
Baseline
Becker, Boris
Borg, Bjorn
Capriati, Jennifer
Center Court
Clay
Connors, Jimmy
Davis Cup
Deuce
Edberg, Stefan
Evert, Chris
Forehand
French Open
Graf, Steffi
Grand Slam
Lendl, Ivan
Lob
Love
Match Point
McEnroe, John
Mixed Doubles
Navratilova, Martina
Sabatini, Gabriela
Seles, Monica
Set
Tiebreaker
U.S. Open
Volley
Wimbledon

Tennis star Ivan Lendl

Boxing

Ali, Muhammad
Ali vs. Frazier
Bell
Belt
Canvas
Clay, Cassius
Corner
Cross
Dempsey vs. Tunney
8 Count
Foreman, George
Frazier, Joe
Hook
Jab
King, Don
KO
Leonard, Sugar Ray
Leonard vs. Duran
Long Count
Louis, Joe
Ring
Robinson, Sugar Ray
Rope A Dope
Split Decision
TKO
Tyson, Mike
Tyson vs. Douglas
Unanimous Decision
Uppercut
Weigh In

Racing

Andretti, Mario
Breeder's Cup
Daytona
Darlington
Formula 1
Foyt, A.J.
Grand Prix
Indy 500
Kentucky Derby
NASCAR
Pace Car
Petty, Richard
Pit Crew
Pit Stop
Secretariat
Shoemaker, Willie
Stewart, Jackie
Stock Car
Triple Crown

South Carolina's Darlington 500

Television

Albert, Marv
Berman, Chris
Buck, Jack
Caray, Harry
Closed Circuit
CNN Sports
Color
Cosell, Howard
Costas, Bob
Dierdorf, Dan
Enberg, Dick
Firestone, Roy
ESPN
Gifford, Frank
Jackson, Keith
King, Larry
Madden, John
McGuire, Al
Michaels, Al
Musburger, Brent

ESPN's popular announcer Chris Berman

Pay Per View
Play By Play
Scully, Vin
Sportscenter
Sports Machine
Storm, Hannah
Valvano, Jim
Vitale, Dick

Stadiums and Arenas

Astrodome
Boston Garden
Candlestick Park
Coliseum (L.A.)
Comiskey Park
Dodger Stadium
Ebbets Field
Fenway Park
Forum (L.A.)
Louisiana Superdome
Madison Square Garden
Soldier Field
Tiger Stadium
Wembley Stadium
Wrigley Field
Yankee Stadium

Tiger Stadium, Detroit, built in 1912

How Did You Do?

0-108: You have two options: start improving your IQ immediately or move to Antarctica.

109-181: You need work, but at least you know something.

182-252: You're well on your way to becoming Sports Literate. Keep up the good effort.

253-325: Your Sports IQ will get you through almost any situation, but beware of the Sports Know-It-All.

325-360: Congratulations! You are officially Sports Literate. Pour yourself a large beer.

About the Authors

Bill Jeakle and Ed Wyatt wrote and published their first successful book, *HOW TO COLLEGE*, during their senior year at Stanford University. Jeakle went on to spend several years directing new business development at Turner Broadcasting, while Wyatt became an Emmy award winning television writer/ producer on several television programs.

They reteamed in 1990 to form Jeakle/Wyatt Productions, a creative venture specializing in book and television project development. They live in Seattle, Washington.